SEARCH FOR SALVATION

Studies in the History and Theology of Cargo Cults

John G. Strelan

Lutheran Publishing House, Adelaide

TO MY FOUR FATHERS —
Pastor Peter G. Strelan
Pastor Rudolph M. Graebner
Doctor Henry P. Hamann
Doctor Martin H. Scharlemann

Printed and Published by
Lutheran Publishing House,
205 Halifax Street, Adelaide, South Australia.

First published April 1977.

ISBN 0 85910 037 5

CONTENTS

FOREWORD

Cargo cults are known to the world as exotic Melanesian movements in which stone-age peoples make what seem to be quite irrational responses to their encounter with Western culture with its technology and wealth. This image has been encouraged by film documentaries and TV programs about bamboo aeroplanes and home-made airstrips, wharves, and warehouses — all built by cult enthusiasts awaiting the cargo that will come from supernatural sources. It is found again in the almost-inevitable passage on such cult movements in the spate of travel books and personal reminiscences on Papua New Guinea. And there are many in this nation (and not only expatriates) who still operate with this stereotype, and who condemn these 'pagan syncretisms or heresies' if they speak from within the national churches or the Christian missions, or these 'stupid retrogressive obstacles to real development' if representing government or the concern for economic advance.

Neither the stereotype, nor the quick theological judgment, nor the developer's condemnation produces genuine understanding of these movements, much less an ability to cope with them if they occur in one's own area. They need to be seen not as freak phenomena in Melanesia, but as local variations of a world-wide religious response of tribal peoples in the course of their interactions with Western societies and the Christian religion for the most part (and to a lesser degree with the Hindu and Buddhist societies of Asia).

The massive response of the tribal peoples of the world to the modern missionary movement from the Christian West over the past two centuries will not be unknown to the readers of this work; it has led increasingly to the establishment of national Christian churches across the world, and not least in Melanesia. What is not so well recognized as yet is that behind the church form of response there lies another extensive reaction in the shape of a vast range of new religious movements, independent in varying degrees of both the missions and churches, and of the indigenous tribal religious systems. The cargo cults of Melanesia are only one form, and even here there are other kinds without the cargo idea, such as Silas Eto's Christian Fellowship Church in the Solomons. Elsewhere in the Pacific, similar new religious movements are still arising (as in Fiji), or are continuing (among New Zealand Maoris from origins going back between sixty and a hundred years). In the Philippines there are hundreds of such movements; in Black Africa there are thousands (mostly of the independent church form but sometimes with cargo ideas); among the Indian tribes of North and South America there are many others.

None of these movements would have arisen if the Christian religion had not been brought to the tribal peoples concerned. To that extent, they are part of Christian history, and in their independent and unorthodox aspects they present the Christian community with a newly-discovered responsibility along what I have called elsewhere a 'new mission and ecumenical front' that stretches across many parts of the world. The first responsibility, however, is to recognize their existence and to take them seriously as authentic religious creations of peoples who are earnestly engaged in what Dr Strelan rightly calls the 'search for salvation'.

It was to accept this responsibility and to set these cargo and other Melanesian cults in the wider world-perspective that the Melanesian Institute for Pastoral and Socio-Economic Service organized the Seminar on Adjustment Movements (as it quite suitably called them) at Lae in July 1976; here I was privileged to join with others ranging from Fiji to Irian Jaya in sustained study of these movements.

At this seminar it became plain how little attempt had been made to understand the distinctively-religious dimension of the Melanesian movements. They were best known to the world through P.M. Worsley's *The Trumpet Shall Sound*, which conveys a great deal of information, emphasizes nationalist political interpretations, and lacks intimate first-hand experience or any recognition of a distinctive religious dimension. Peter Lawrence's detailed and sympathetic anthropological case-studies, especially of the Madang area and the Yali movement, naturally go deeper. And there have been many other works of varying value from the social sciences. Dr Strelan has provided a convenient survey of the external facts about the various cargo cult movements, including some information not previously published, and has also outlined the various anthropological and other theories for their interpretation. He then seeks for a viewpoint that will do justice to their religious concerns, without denying all the non-religious factors so extensively discussed by others. His double conclusion is of the utmost importance: that these movements are authentic reflections of the basic religious beliefs and mythology of Melanesians, and that they also form a genuine search for salvation on a new model that has been influenced by the Christian contact.

It is only after the religious form and content of a movement has been understood, and the religious elements in the aspirations of its members laid bare, that theological evaluation can be attempted. It is this final task that is Dr Strelan's main concern, but he approaches it in the only legitimate way: through the study of these movements as religions, after acknowledging that they will be many other things as well. At this stage he draws on two of the very few theological approaches already in existence: the doctoral study by F. Steinbauer (rather inaccessible in German) and the small but seminal study by G. Oosterwal (from a little-known United States source); both authors have been missionaries in Melanesia. In contrast to Oosterwal's more eschatological emphasis, Dr Strelan takes the basic human and religious concern in the cargo cults to be the search for salvation here and now. He then applies a systematic critique to this one theme, using biblical theology (with which he is well equipped) in some depth. This provides a theological interpretation that enables him to deal with the misunderstandings of Christian eschatology in these movements. This is the heart of this book, and it is a valuable new contribution.

On this basis he can then expose the total misunderstandings implicit in some earlier Catholic and Lutheran (and, no doubt, other) responses to cargo cults. Perhaps only a Lutheran author can effectively demonstrate how previous attitudes have often been anti-Lutheran in effect! It is somewhat ironic, for example, to find that revelations through dreams can be rapidly dismissed as tricks of Satan in spite of the conspicuous place of dreams at critical junctures in the Christian Scriptures, and of the solidly-biblical nature of the Lutheran tradition. Clearly, even Western theologians have some more thinking to do at this point, and Dr Strelan's suggestions for the response of the churches to these cults deserve the closest attention by those concerned.

It should also be noted that Dr Strelan stands in a notable tradition; in the missionary community, it is Lutherans who above all others have given serious and scholarly attention — even if not always with the necessary sympathetic understanding — to these movements. In the early 1940s it was a Lutheran, Rudolf Inselmann, who wrote a master's thesis on the Letub cult, and who was able to entitle a small booklet: 'Letub is a call for justice in the jungle of New Guinea'. Steinbauer and many others referred to in the notes for this work have been Lutherans, and extensive unpublished reports from Lutheran sources have also been drawn upon for this study — for example, J.F. Wagner's 'The Outgrowth and Development of the Cargo Cult', a paper in 1964 that runs to 203 pages. I can also refer to another master's dissertation, submitted to the University of Aberdeen in 1976 by a Lutheran missionary, B.M. Schwarz; this is a penetrating study of the deep symbolism of the cargo idea which is so often misunderstood outside these cults as a crassly-materialistic search for affluence rather than as a deep longing for fullness of humanity and for equality with, and acceptance by, whites and other peoples in the world.

Dr Strelan's work combines this kind of understanding with a stringent theological critique, and in so doing points the way forward for further study and for practical action.

Department of Religious
Studies
University of Aberdeen,
Scotland
February 1977.

Harold W. Turner
Director,
Project for the Study of
New Religious Movements
in Primal Societies.

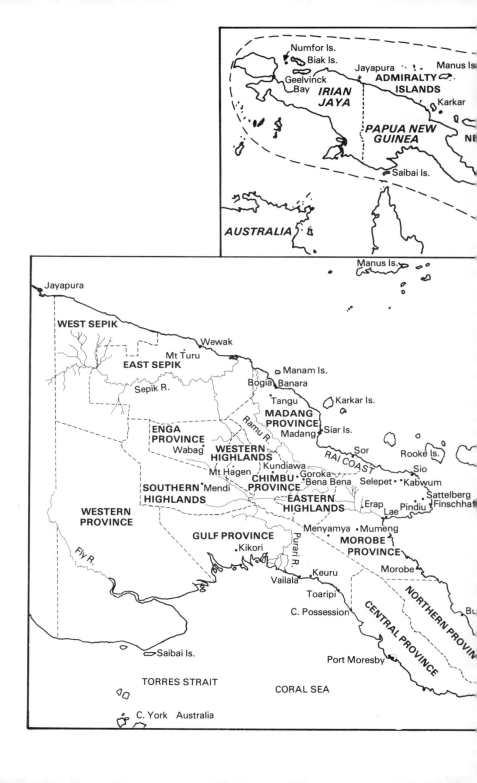

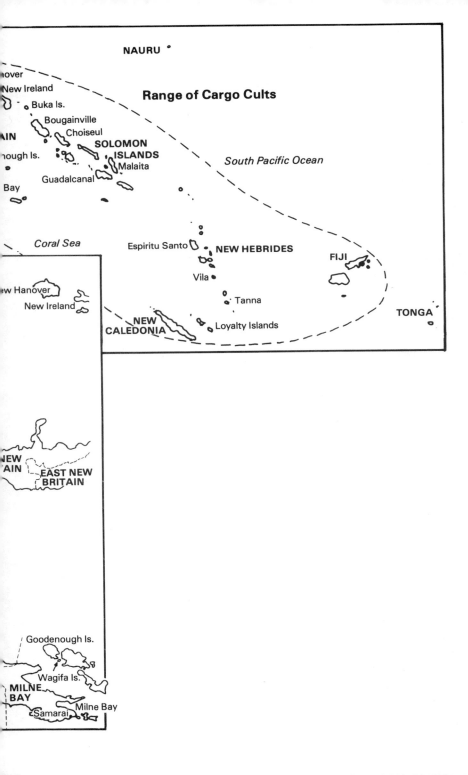

INTRODUCTION

The region of the world known as Melanesia, of which Papua New Guinea is a large part, has been fertile soil for the growth of many indigenous religious movements. These movements are described in anthropological and sociological literature by such adjectives as nativistic, prophetic, adjustment, millenarian, messianic, and so forth. In popular parlance, they are known as cargo cults.

Analytically, the term 'cargo cults' should be used only to refer to those movements which emphasize and employ religious and magical doctrines and rituals to explain and achieve their purposes. The name, however, is commonly applied to any movement which contains the expectation of the receipt of material or spiritual goods by any means which do not fully meet Western criteria for the 'right' way of achieving the good life. This misuse of the term is unfortunate, but not fatal. Far more serious is the fact that in government and church circles (especially in the latter) the name 'cargo cults' has become a pejorative; if one wants to condemn, reject, and dismiss a movement with a somewhat contemptuous shrug, one calls it a cargo cult.

Nevertheless, I have chosen to retain the name 'cargo cults', and to use it as a generic term for the movements viewed collectively, simply because it is the name in popular use, and also because the phrase has entered the vocabulary of Melanesian Pidgin in the form *kago kalt*. To designate a concrete, individual movement or cult I have used the expression 'cargo movement'. A third term which is employed in the chapters which follow is 'cargoism'. This useful word refers chiefly to the cargo beliefs, the cargo myths and ideology, the cargo philosophy if you like. Recognition of the fact that there is such a thing as cargoism helps one to avoid the cargo/non-cargo dichotomy which seems to have vitiated some discussions of Melanesian religious movements. Cargoism in Melanesia is endemic; it exists even when and where there is no overt cargo movement or cargo activity. Cargoism can provide the dynamic for a modern developmental project just as easily as it can undergird a classical cargo movement. In one sense, this book is concerned more with cargoism than it is with cargo cults.

Cargo cults have to do with Melanesian concepts of power, status, wealth, and the good life. Characteristic of these cults is the expectation of a radical change in the social, economic, and even the cosmic, order. There will be a new life, a new life-style, a new world which will be patterned after the way things were thought to have been before, in the beginning. A certain amount of ritualistic activity is required to usher in the anticipated new order. Usually the return of the ancestors is expected. Sometimes it is said that they will be led by a messiah-like figure, a folk-hero from the historical or mythical past. He and the ancestors will bring with them 'cargo'. This word is an inadequate translation of the Pidgin word *kago*. Included in the concept of *kago* may be such things as food, clothing, and other goods, economic development, money, technological advancement, release from oppression, knowledge, peace, social justice, status — in fact, whatever is thought to be necessary for the good life. In theological terms, *kago* may be regarded as a synonym for what some world-religions call 'salvation'.

Many of the external aspects of a cargo movement appear strange, unusual, and even a little ridiculous to a Western observer. Unfortunately, these are the features which make newspaper headlines and which tend to colour the thinking and attitudes of many non-Melanesians who try to interpret cargo cults. The bizarre features of the cults, together with their tendency to rise rapidly and decline abruptly, seem to have led some Western observers to the conclusion that cargo cults are nothing more than outbreaks of a kind of madness which periodically seizes frustrated, primitive peoples. The idea is propounded that, with opposition from the government and the church, supported by a planned educational drive and economic development, cargo cults and cargo thinking will gradually disappear. These, however, are oversimplified solutions based on a superficial analysis of a complex problem. Such proposals indicate a lack of understanding of the very basic and deeply-human dynamics which are involved; they fail, furthermore, to take into account the sheer persistence of cargo cults despite one hundred years of opposition on the part of government and church.

There is a growing body of evidence to support the thesis that cargo cults are serious attempts to respond to deep-rooted imperatives in the Melanesian cultures.[1] They are the external, ritualistic expression of genuinely-indigenous religious beliefs and hopes which existed long before the arrival of the Gospel, and which will continue to exist unless there is a radical (i.e., at the very roots) change in Melanesian religious orientation.

Cargo cults and cargo ideology have presented a direct challenge to Christianity ever since the first missionary set foot on Melanesia. The Christian churches generally have been slow to recognize the challenge, and even slower to respond to it in a positive way. A survey of the available published literature on cargo cults reveals that these religious movements have been described and analysed and interpreted from the point of view of anthropology, sociology, and psychiatry, but studies made from a religious or specifically-Christian perspective are scarce, and most of the little that has been done is unavailable in published form. Christians in Melanesia and in other parts of the world need to know more about cargo cults, about their ideology, their roots, their goals. A Christian analysis of cargo cults is needed so that Christians can at least try to understand what it is that makes a cargo cultist believe and hope and act as he does.

Such information and interpretation is what this book is intended to provide, if only in a limited way. These pages are addressed, in the first instance, to Christians whose culture is called 'Western'. Information is offered here on cargo cults in their historical setting, together with an analysis of the characteristic elements of the cargo ideology. My aim has been to offer a view of cargo cults which is both sympathetic and critical. Melanesian Christians will perhaps learn something from this book, despite its frequent lack of perceptiveness and ignorance of vital aspects of Melanesian religious life and thought.

Last of all, these chapters are addressed to any thoughtful reader, Christian or not, who is willing to take seriously the religious phenomenon called cargo cults.

Chapter 1

FROM MANSREN TO MAMBU

The written history of cargo cults in Melanesia begins soon after the middle of the 19th century. Nobody knows how many movements occurred in Melanesia prior to 1860. Nor does anyone know exactly how many movements have erupted in the period between 1860 and the present. It is possible to distinguish up to two hundred movements since 1860; however, to that number must be added those movements which are mentioned in the notes and journals of missionaries, anthropologists, and government officers, but of which no details exist in writing. And to that total must be added those movements which are remembered only in oral history, together with those which have simply been forgotten.

It may be said with certainty that outbreaks of cargo movements have occurred regularly in Melanesia during the past 100 years. Furthermore, it is certain that the movements have not been confined to only one or two areas in Melanesia; a geographical plotting of cargo activities indicates that such activity has taken place in every part of Melanesia, from Irian Jaya in the north and west, to New Caledonia in the south, and Fiji in the east.

The brief history which is offered in this and the following chapter cuts across geographical boundaries, and adheres closely to a chronological order, except in a few cases where it has seemed desirable to trace a movement through to its conclusion. The era between 1860 and the present may be divided conveniently into three parts: (1) the period before World War I; (2) the period between World War I and World War II; and (3) the period from the start of World War II in Melanesia to the present day. From each of these three periods, one or two movements have been chosen as representatives of the many. These typical movements are described in more detail than the others. One of the features of cargo movements is that though they occur in widely-separated areas, they have many characteristics in common. Consequently, after reading a description of a new movement, the reader gets the uneasy feeling that he has read it all before; a good description of one movement seems to fit many others.

The First Period: 1860-1914

The first extant written report of cargoism (as distinct from an actual cargo movement) comes from Irian Jaya. Missionaries from Germany had arrived in the area on February 5, 1855. In 1857 they reported hearing a strange story about a man called Mansren, about a *Konoor* or herald, and about a *Koreri*, a golden age.

The Mansren Myth

Manamakeri (so one version of the story goes) was an ugly bachelor afflicted with an infectious skin disease.[1] One night he surprised a young man in the act of tapping juice for palm wine from his favourite tree. The youth was none other than Sampari, the Morning Star. He would die if he did not reach his home in the sky before dawn. In exchange for his release, Sampari gave Manamakeri magical powers which would enable him to have all his wishes fulfilled.

Soon afterwards, a big dance was held to welcome home some men from a trading expedition. Manamakeri, of course, was not permitted to attend the dance, but he climbed a tree to watch from a distance. He threw some *bintanggur* fruit at the breasts of a young girl, with the result that she became pregnant. The girl, Ninggai (also known as Insoraki), gave birth to a son, Konoor (bringer of peace). When the girl's family learnt of the apparent *mésalliance* between the old man Manamakeri and the young virgin, they destroyed all their gardens, houses, and canoes, and left the little island on which they had lived. Only Manamakeri, his wife, and the child remained behind. But the special powers which Manamakeri had been given enabled the trio to survive. The old man changed himself into a handsome youth by discarding his skin in the flames of an ironwood fire. He took a new name: Mansren Manggundi (the Lord Himself). When his family complained of loneliness, Mansren created four groups of people to live on an island which he had formed in the middle of Geelvinck Bay. Mansren gave to these people their customs and taboos. He ruled over the populace, cured their sicknesses, healed their diseases, and provided for all their needs. But a woman whose child had died incited the people to rebel against Mansren, and he took his departure westward. It is generally thought that he journeyed on until he came to Holland.

Mansren, however, would return after seven generations, so it was said. When he did return, the golden age, called the *Koreri*, would begin. This word *Koreri* actually consists of two syllables: *Ko* (we) and *rer* (take off old skin). Hence *Koreri* literally means:

'We take off our old skins and put on new ones'. The age of *Koreri* would begin when a coconut which Mansren had planted at the place where he was living would grow into a huge tree reaching to heaven. Eventually the tree would overbalance and fall down until it touched an island in Geelvinck Bay. The *Konoor* would then descend the trunk — and the *Koreri* would have arrived: the old would become young; the dead would return; everybody would enjoy perfect health; there would be no shortage of money, food, weapons, women, or ornaments; no one would have to work or pay taxes.

About 10 years after this myth had been brought to the attention of Western specialists, a movement broke out in which the most conspicuous figure was a man who called himself Konoor. He claimed to have had a vision, as a result of which people began to revolt against the normal rules of daily life. Work was abandoned. Men danced all night and slept all day or gathered food. This went on for about a month. Every time a dance was held, it was possible to recognize a performance of the myth of Mansren. But at first the missionaries did not connect the ritual dance with the myth. They had been told only the first part of the myth; they had not learnt the ending — that Mansren would return to usher in the *Koreri*, the age of deliverance, peace, and prosperity, the age of salvation.

The myth of Mansren became the dynamic for a number of movements in Irian Jaya during the next 100 hundred years. In each of these movements a man or woman arose, claiming to be a *Konoor*. The imminent arrival of Mansren would be announced, together with the impending inauguration of the *Koreri*. The more important of these movements will be noted in their proper chronological order.

The Tuka Cult

In 1877 there arose on the island of Fiji a cult which, as Burridge remarks:

> furnishes us with most of the classical characteristics of a Melanesian cargo cult.[2]

The government of Fiji ignored the movement at first; only in 1885 was it discovered that the movement — known as the Tuka Cult — had become very active under the leadership of one Ndugmoi. This man took for himself the name Navosavakandua, the title which was applied by the local people to the Chief Justice of Fiji, and interpreted to mean 'He who speaks once'. Navosavakandua claimed that he had learnt by revelation that the ancestors were about to return and to usher in a new order in which the present order would be reversed: the Europeans would become the servants of the Fijians; chiefs would serve commoners; the old lands and the old freedoms would be restored; the golden age of plenty would begin; believers would be granted perpetual youth and eternal life. Bottles of water were sold for £1; the water, it was said, came from the fountain of life, which was equated by some with the Christian heaven. Unbelievers (those who did not follow Ndugmoi) were condemned to a place not unlike the Christian hell. Followers were organized along military lines; bands of men were drilled by ex-policemen, and Ndugmoi expected military salutes to be given him.

The Tuka Cult flourished until the leaders were arrested. Navosavakandua had named the day on which the ancestors would return. His followers abandoned fields and crops, and made veiled threats against the government. The prophet was arrested, brought to trial, and banished to the island of Rotuma. Ten years later, as he was returning from exile, Navosavakandua died. But, 50 years after his death, people were still hoping for his return.

The Prophet Tokeriu

Tokeriu was a prophet from the Milne Bay area of Papua New Guinea.[3] He claimed that he was inspired by a spirit who lived in a sacred tree. Tokeriu asserted that he had visited *Hiyoyoa*, the other world, where he had learnt that a new age was coming. The arrival of this new age would involve drastic changes in the social and cosmic structures: a terrible cataclysm, accompanied by volcanic eruptions, earthquakes, and floods, would strike the unbelievers. Afterwards, the prophet predicted, the winds would change and blow from the south-east, bringing fair weather and causing the fields to fill with taro and other crops. Trees would groan under their load of fruit. A ship would come into port; on board would be the ancestral dead who had come to visit their families. The faithful who wished to survive, and to experience this wonderful time, were to keep themselves from being contaminated by anything European.

Tokeriu's message met with a ready response. Hundreds of pigs — the reservoir of the society's wealth, and of the greatest social value — were slaughtered and eaten. All work was suspended. After a period of frustrated waiting, the prophet's followers became disillusioned and threatened to kill him. The government intervened and sentenced Tokeriu to two years' imprisonment in Samarai gaol. The movement died, but the hopes engendered lived on.

The Madang Revolt and the Manup-Kilibob Myth

In 1903 a virulent anti-government movement arose in the Madang district of Papua New Guinea. Plans to kill most of the 26 German government officials and missionaries in the Madang area in July 1904 were divulged at the last minute by an informer named Nalon. Nalon told his brother Fungas of the plot; Fungas in turn informed his employer, the medical officer, who quickly passed the information on to the District Officer, Wilhelm Stückhardt. The conspirators were rounded up and imprisoned in Madang or returned to Siar. Seven of the leaders, representing the seven Siar patrilineages, were executed; later, another three men who had been imprisoned in Rabaul were returned to Madang and executed. The final act in the insurrection drama came in 1912, when most of the people of Siar were exiled to Menderei, and their lands alienated.[4]

This series of actions led to a drastic reinterpretation of an old and widespread myth known as the Manup-Kilibob myth.[5] The myth was well known already in 1871, when the Russian scientist and scholar Mikloucho-Maclay landed on the Rai Coast. The people identified the Russian with Anut, the god of creation, or possibly with one of Anut's two sons, Manup or Kilibob.

According to a common version of the myth of which Manup and Kilibob are the principals, the two brothers quarrelled and separated. Manup, the originator of love magic, sorcery, and war, made a canoe and sailed north from Karkar Island. The younger brother, Kilibob, made a large canoe, and then created men, pigs, dogs, food plants, and artifacts, all of which he took on board with him. He sailed to Madang, and then on down the Rai Coast, creating new islands and reefs as he went. At each coastal village he put a man ashore, and gave him the power of speech as well as plants, bows and arrows, stone axes, rain and ritual formulas. Kilibob himself sailed on and settled in the south-east.

The myth foretells that Kilibob will one day return to New Guinea. At the time of his return, there will be an eclipse of the sun and violent volcanic eruptions which will bury gardens in ashes. After this, the country will be devastated by war and cannibalism, until finally the brothers are reconciled.

After the failure of the Madang Revolt, the Manup-Kilibob myth was reinterpreted in such a way that the Melanesians were said to have acted foolishly and so to have lost the good life by their own stupidity. Kilibob's military superiority and more effective technology were gifts from the gods. That was why the European had guns, while the Melanesian was forced to be content with bows and arrows. The only hope for the future lay in the early return of the two brothers. Their return would lead to a war which would soon be over. Then peace and equality would once more prevail.

The anthropologist Peter Lawrence, whose studies of cargo cults in the Southern Madang district are regarded as definitive, has identified five distinct, but related, cargo movements, all based on variations and developments of the Manup-Kilibob myth.[6] The most recent of the movements, centring on the charismatic figure of Yali Singina, arose in the period between 1946 and 1950, and was still gathering adherents 25 years later.

Movements in the Torres Straits and on Buka Island

During the years 1913-1915 there arose in the extreme south of Melanesia a cult known as the German Wislin Movement.[7] This cult was centred on Saibai Island in the Torres Strait group. The doctrine of German Wislin was similar to that of the earlier Milne Bay movement led by Tokeriu, but with the important difference that the ancestors would not initiate a millennial period of agricultural prosperity, but would bring an abundance of European goods.

About this time, one of the earliest-known cargo movements in what is now the North Solomons Province arose at Lontis on Buka Island.[8] Few details are known of the movement. Its leaders, Novite and Muling, were arrested by German government officials and taken to Morobe, where Novite died. Muling was not heard of again until 1932, when he joined a man named Pako in another movement. Muling, who claimed to be a relative of the sun and the moon, prophesied that a tidal wave would come and sweep away many villages. He also foretold the arrival of a ship bearing axes, food, tobacco, motor vehicles, and firearms. The ship's white crew were thought to be the returning ancestors of the Bukas. Pako and Muling were taken into custody, and the movement subsequently died.

The Taro Cult

The period immediately prior to World War I saw the outbreak of a number of prophet-led movements in north-east Papua. In 1912, for example, the Baigona Cult, led by a man named Maine, gathered a number of adherents. [9]

But the most important and most influential of the cults which arose about this time was the Taro Cult, promoted by a prophet named Buninia.[10] He claimed that he had been visited by the spirit of his father, who was accompanied by a crowd of other spirits, all of whom were eating taro. The spirit instructed his son in the rites of a new cult which was intended to increase the taro crop. Buninia announced a special ritual which was to be applied to gardening activities. An important feature of this ritual was spirit-possession accompanied by convulsions. The first participants to become possessed were regarded as Taro-men or Taro-spirits, and were said to have special authority over the group.

It is worth noting that, although the Taro Cult promised vast improvements in certain areas of life, no drastic changes were expected. There were no overt millennial tendencies in the movement. By concentrating on the plant food which was not only the staple diet of the people but also the central character in many aetiological myths of the society, the Taro Cult hoped to find answers to both chronic and newly-arisen social and political problems.[11]

This brings to a conclusion our survey of the first historical period. We have seen that cargo cults or related movements are known to have occurred in the period under review in widely-separated areas within Melanesia. The fact that there are no reports of cargo cults from many other parts of Melanesia during this period should not lead to the conclusion that no movements took place in those areas. Some districts, such as the populous highlands region of Papua New Guinea, had not yet been contacted by Europeans; hence, even if cargo movements had occurred there, there would be no written reports available.

The Second Period: 1915-1941

The Vailala Madness

The first major cargo movement known to have erupted after World War I was the one inaptly named the Vailala Madness.[12] This movement was first reported in 1919, but it had probably begun several years earlier. All the villages, from Vailala in Papua as far eastward as Keuru, were affected. The coincidence of the ending of the war of 1914-1918 with the outbreak of the Vailala Madness may not be entirely coincidental; the supposed language of the Madness leaders when they were speaking in tongues was 'Djaman'.

The originator of the Vailala movement is thought to have been a man named Evara, who first experienced the Madness while in a state of shock brought on by the death of his father. Evara prophesied the coming of a huge steamer carrying the spirits of the ancestors, who would bring with them a fascinating variety of European and native goods. To obtain these goods, it would be necessary to expel all Europeans. Evara wanted his people to have white skins like the skins of the returning ancestors.

A vital factor in the success of the movement was control of the dead (who are, of course, not dead, but alive). To achieve this, three things were necessary. First, mortuary feasts had to be held for the ancestors; the function of these feasts was to hasten the return of the ancestors who would usher in the golden age. Secondly, prohibitions against stealing, adultery, and disobedience had to be strictly observed. Thirdly, heat or *ahea* had to be generated. The attempt to produce heat resulted in the physical disturbances which led to the movement being dubbed the 'Madness'. European influences could be seen in the rituals: flag-raising and military drills were encouraged, as was also the practice of donning white clothes and sitting at tables in a ritualistic manner. But the most obvious and startling manifestations of the movement were spirit-possession and speaking in tongues.

The Vailala Madness continued with diminishing effects until about 1931. At that time, organized activity apparently ceased. But the memory of the expectations which had been engendered by the movement lingered on. In time, the era of the Madness passed into legend. Investigations, made a decade after the movement had apparently petered out, revealed that the people had come to believe that the things which had been prophesied and promised in 1919 had actually taken place. It was narrated how, in that marvellous time, the ground shook, and trees swayed, and flowers sprang up in profusion; the ancestors came, riding on bicycles and walking on the beach; long-dead favourite dogs and pigs returned to life. And the steamers which everyone had expected had actually come; some who later told the story had seen it through the mists with their own eyes. [13] Forty years later, an anthropologist who did field-work among one group of people (the Toaripi) who had been affected by the Madness, reported:

> Among the Toaripi the cult never really disappeared: the seizures, elaborate mortuary feasts, cult houses, and so on, appeared less frequently; but the belief that a new, valuable and true message had been imparted remained as strong as ever. [14]

Ronovuro

The 1920s saw the rise of a number of cargo movements throughout Melanesia. Ronovuro, a prophet who lived at Espiritu Santo in the New Hebrides, in 1923 foretold the coming of a great flood, as well as the return of the dead with white skins. [15] The dead, he said, would land on the island from a ship loaded with rice and other foods. But, since the Europeans would seek to prevent the unloading of the goods, one man, representative of the rest, must be offered as a victim.

Consequently, a planter, Mr R.O.D. Clapcott, was shot, his body mutilated, and parts of it eaten. The movement came to an abrupt halt when the government intervened swiftly and powerfully; Ronovuro and two accomplices were executed. However, by 1937 the movement had again gathered momentum. It reached a peak in 1947 when a so-called 'naked' cult spread far and wide.

The *Eemasang* Movement

The Finschhafen-Sattelberg area of the Morobe Province was the scene of the *eemasang* movement, which began in 1927.[16] This religious movement was initiated by Christian leaders in an attempt to revive and strengthen the flagging faith and life of the people. The leader of *eemasang* in its early stages was Selembe.

Simultaneously with the development of *eemasang*, there arose a cargo movement under the leadership of three men from the Wemola tribe: Mutari, Tutumang, and (later) Tikombe. Their central claim was that they had discovered the European secret of the production of money. If believers were injected with 'money-water' (using the sharpened point of an umbrella as a syringe), they would have the power to pull money out of the air.

By 1929-30 it was found that, in many areas, the *eemasang* movement had merged with the cargo movement, with the consequence that prayer, confession, and church services were used as part of the ritual attempt to obtain money and other possessions in a magical manner. *Eemasang* with its accretions of cargoism continued until 1938, when the Christians of the area formally renounced it and returned to the church.

Various Movements in Irian Jaya

In 1928 a cargo movement based on the Mansren myth broke out in Irian Jaya.[17] This movement was headed by Wasjari, who claimed to be king of Papua. Wasjari said that he had had a vision in which Mansren appeared to him in human form, saying that in 10 days he planned to return to Irian Jaya and bring with him salvation from the troubles of life. Wasjari prophesied that the world would turn dark and then sink, but the prophet himself would build a boat (designed by Mansren), and this ship would rescue all the faithful.

The government intervened and imprisoned Wasjari. This action led to another outbreak of cult activity. A new prophet arose. He predicted that Mansren would return in a ship two miles long. Wasjari was released from prison and promptly became the focal point of another Mansren movement. Just as promptly he was gaoled once more, and hopes went off the boil.

21

Two other pre-war movements in Irian Jaya may be noted. In 1934 a *Konoor* predicted the coming of Mansren in a four-funnelled steamer. His return would inaugurate the *Koreri*, the golden age. In 1936 a prophet claimed to have seen Mansren arriving on earth in the company of the queen of heaven. The *Konoor* in this case was Njawamos. He died in prison in 1938. His death brought to an end that particular wave of movements; but outbreaks of cargo activity fuelled by the Mansren myth continued, and still continue in various parts of Irian Jaya up to the present day.[18]

The revitalization of the golden-age myth was symptomatic of a general unrest in Melanesia in the 1930s. In this period reports of cargo activities came in from all quarters.

Among the Baining of New Britain

In 1929-30 the myth of the golden age spread among the Baining of New Britain.[19] An earthquake was expected to destroy all Europeans, as well as sceptics among the native population. Mountains would crumble into valleys, thus creating a huge plain covered with gardens and orchards which would bear fruit in prodigious quantities. All the dead, including long-dead dogs and pigs, would be resurrected.

Pako and Sanop on Buka

At Buka in the North Solomons Province a movement which had petered out 20 years earlier was revived in 1931-32.[20] The prophet of the cult predicted that an imminent deluge would swallow up all Europeans, after which a ship laden with goods of every kind would arrive. But this ship would berth only when the people had reached the end of their own resources and supplies. So, all work ceased, and a concerted effort was made to consume all existing provisions. Despite the arrest and imprisonment of the leaders, the movement continued for some years, spurred on by reports that one of the leaders, Pako, had risen from the dead.

In 1934 a successor to Pako arose: Sanop, the self-styled mouthpiece of Pako. According to Sanop, the arrival of the ship loaded with goods would coincide with the resurrection of the dead. Once again, people abandoned their fields and gardens, and began to worship and to offer sacrifices at the graves of their forebears in order to hasten their return. Eventually Sanop was arrested and imprisoned. The Pako-Sanop movement continued spasmodically for the next few years. It was finally crushed by the Japanese occupation authorities in 1942.

Pokokoqoro's Movement

Pokokoqoro was an ex-policeman who began a cargo movement on the little island of Vasu in the Tabataba district of Choiseul in the Solomons. [21] He held before his people the vision of a glorious future, complete with a ship filled with a cargo of rice, tinned food, and other forms of wealth. The prophet's followers eagerly helped with the construction of storehouses to receive the expected goods. By persuading the people to invest with him sums of money ranging from £10 to £30, Pokokoqoro was able to maintain a show of affluence for some time. When no ship arrived and funds began to dwindle, Pokokoqoro shifted his headquarters to Varese. His movement was vigorously opposed by the Catholic and Methodist churches, but Pokokoqoro's activities continued to do much economic, social, and religious mischief until it ended in disillusionment for all in 1940.

Cargo Movements in the Morobe Province

The return of the dead bringing food, wealth, and a new age was proclaimed also by the prophet Upikno at Gitua among the Kalasa people. [22] In 1933 Upikno began to advise people to confess their sins, pray to God, and get rid of all native clothes and goods. His followers proceeded to kill all their pigs, eat all their yams, and destroy all their clothing, garden tools, axes, and knives. Their explicit expectation was that, at sunset one evening, a cloud of light would appear, and the cargo ship, manned by the ancestors, would arrive. When nothing resulted from all the activity, the doctrine of the movement was reversed: no European clothing was to be worn; people must revert to their native grass skirts and other wearing apparel. Eventually the believers grew tired of waiting, and the movement died. But the hopes and expectations remained alive.

In 1932-34 a man in the Markham Valley began to have visions of his dead father and of Jesus Christ. [23] He said that the arrival of the ancestors would bring about the end of the world. Many people listened to the prophet, but, before the movement could gather momentum, the government arrested the leaders.

The following year another prophet, Marafi, arose. [24] He claimed to have received all power from Satan, who had once enabled the prophet to visit the kingdom of the dead. Marafi had been informed that a cataclysm, which would spare only the faithful, would be followed by the return of the dead. Since these returning ancestors would bring rice, meat, and other foods, work was no longer necessary. The people heard the prophet gladly. But when he was arrested, normal patterns of life and work were resumed. The Marafi movement smouldered on, however, at least throughout 1936. The unusual feature of this particular movement was the leader's claim that he received his power and authority from Satan. The usual pattern, in those movements which were influenced by Christian ideas, was for the leader or prophet to claim inspiration, power, and authority from Jesus Christ or the Holy Spirit.

Mambu the Prophet

The Madang Province witnessed the eruption of a number of cargo movements in the period 1930-1940. Unfortunately, very little is known of these movements apart from obscure and tantalizing references in the reports of missionaries and patrol officers. More information, however, is available on the Mambu movement, which began in 1937-38 and continued to be influential even after the conclusion of World War II.

Mambu was a prophet from Bogia in the Madang Province.[25] Toward the end of 1937 he returned from a spell of contract-labour in Rabaul. Soon after his arrival at the Bogia Catholic mission station, he did several strange things which attracted attention to himself, and soon after he left the station for his home village, Apingam. There he was rejected by his own people. He then moved to the settlements of the Tangu, where some people received him, and he succeeded in collecting a sum of money. The resident missionary was absent at the time, but when he returned from patrol he took immediate action against Mambu. The money which Mambu had collected was recovered and restored to the donors. Mambu was ordered to leave Tangu immediately.

From the Tangu, Mambu went to the Banara hinterland, and there he began his cult activities in earnest. He persuaded the people that the return of the dead would transform their lives. Europeans, Mambu said, had exploited the people, but the hour of retribution was at hand. The ancestors, who lived inside Manam volcano, were preparing and shipping goods to New Guinea for the use of the New Guineans; however, every time a shipment came in, the Europeans seized it for their own use. This, however, would not happen again, for the goods had been made and were stored in the volcano, and the ancestors themselves were about to deliver the cargo to the rightful recipients.

Mambu developed a full-blown cargo movement. He introduced his own ritual of baptism which would give men a share in the good things to come. Men and women appeared before him, shed their clothes, and had their genitals sprinkled with water. Mambu insisted that the ancestors were not pleased with traditional dress, and that European-style clothes should be worn. Traditional clothes were ritually buried, with Mambu making the sign of the cross over the burial-pits.

The Mambu movement caused a great deal of concern to missionaries and government officers. In the end, Mambu was arrested and imprisoned at Bogia; later, he was taken in chains to Madang. By June 1938 the movement which Mambu had initiated had, to all outward appearances, collapsed. What eventually became of Mambu is not clear. Perhaps he lived in obscurity for years; perhaps he died. His myth, however, lives on.[26] In the myth, Mambu is a hero who went to Sydney and learnt the secrets of the white man's wealth. After many adventures he returned to New Guinea, where he was arrested by jealous government authorities. But even in gaol Mambu was master: he came and went freely, and performed several miracles.

All in all, the Mambu of myth is far more important than the Mambu of history. The anthropologist Kenelm Burridge, who has made a detailed and perceptive study of the Mambu movement, observes that a close connection exists between Mambu and the influential post-war prophet Yali, of whom we shall hear more later. Burridge believes that Yali met with instant acceptance because he had 'revived and re-echoed the Mambu myth'.[27] The Mambu myth gave Yali his initial authority, at least among the Tangu. Later, of course, Yali himself became the central character in the Yali myth, which in turn gave the Yali movement its own authority and dynamic. But behind the myth of Yali and the myth of Mambu lies the myth of Manup and Kilibob.

In the late 1930s the Madang Province was the stage for a number of movements based on the Manup-Kilibob myth. These activities came to a head in several movements which began prior to the outbreak of World War II, but which reached full flower during and after the war. In Irian Jaya another Mansren movement started in 1939. Since these movements reached their peak only during and after World War II, they are included in the third part of this historical survey.

Chapter 2

FROM LETUB TO ?

The Third Period: 1942-

The outbreak of World War II in distant Europe acted as a signal, as it were, for the emergence of a whole series of cargo movements in various parts of Melanesia. The arrival of Japanese occupation forces in 1942, and the subsequent fighting between the Japanese and the allies, were traumatic experiences for the people of Melanesia. Perhaps even more significant in terms of cargo thinking was the sudden influx of huge quantities of equipment and goods, accompanied by hordes of friendly soldiers, both black and white, who tended to act more in line with the traditional concept of 'brother'. There can be no doubt that the experiences of the people during and immediately after the war had at least something to do with the proliferation of cargo cults during this period. The 35-40 cargo movements mentioned in this chapter represent only those movements which were reported in some detail; an uncounted number of other movements occurred, but their story will become generally known only when the oral history of the area is written.

Movements in the Madang Province

Letub and Tagarab

The Letub Cult, which was most active in the Madang district just prior to the Japanese occupation, was based on the Manup-Kilibob myth.[1] This myth had been revised in such a way that Jesus-Manup became the deity and culture-hero of the people of Madang, while Adam and Eve were the culture-heroes of the Europeans. The Jews, it was said, held Jesus-Manup in heaven (in or above Sydney). The Letub ritual was designed to free Jesus-Manup from his bondage so that he could return to Papua New Guinea with his ships and cargo, and supervise the distribution of the goods.

In the Letub Cult, invocations were made to the ancestors at the village cemeteries. Planting of gardens ceased and many pigs were killed. The cult dance which, like most dances in coastal areas, had to be purchased from its owners, spread rapidly. A characteristic feature of the Letub dance was the general shaking and other uncontrolled antics of the performers. These shaking fits were adopted not only as part of the dance but also as a general condition of the cult devotees. While in this state, the leaders were better able to receive messages from the ancestors concerning the future, and especially concerning the arrival of cargo.

In 1942, while the Letub Cult was in full swing, another movement began at Milguk in the Madang hinterland. The leader was an ex-policeman named Tagarab, a man feared for his great strength and quick temper.[2] Basing his doctrine on a version of the Manup-Kilibob myth, Tagarab declared that the missionaries had cunningly taught the people to pray to a fraud, thus deflecting the people's prayers from the true cargo deity to one who could not possibly help them. Because of this deception, God-Kilibob was going to drive out the Europeans and send the spirits of the dead, disguised as Japanese, to bring cargo to the people. At this time, skins would turn from black to white, and there would be storms and earthquakes to herald the new era which was emerging.

Tagarab insisted that the people continue with the outward forms of religious life. The Ten Commandments were to be obeyed to the letter; fighting was to cease; love magic and adultery was to be eliminated. Hymns were to be sung, prayers offered, and sermons preached — but the worship was to be directed to the true cargo deity, not to the false god which the missionaries had tried to foist on the people. Storehouses were built, and daily offerings to the ancestors were made in cemeteries. In August 1942 Tagarab announced that the arrival of the cargo was imminent. People waited with bated breath; however, when nothing happened, many followers began to lose faith in their leader. The movement died when Tagarab retreated with the Japanese to the Sepik. Tagarab had collaborated with the Japanese, but in the end they shot him for treachery.

Kukuaik

Kukuaik was a revival movement begun on Karkar Island in the Madang Province in 1941. A missionary, who visited the island in the immediate aftermath of the movement, described it in its origins as a 'sane procedure to discuss difficulties, settle quarrels, confess sins, and be edified by the Word of God'.[3] It so happened that, at the time when Kukuaik began in the congregations, some unusual phenomena were observed in nature: extreme drought, an influenza epidemic, blood-red sunsets, meteors, comets, bright stars, strange mirages, and mysterious lights. People had dreams and visions. The result of all this was that women and men flocked to church meetings, devotions, and services. Only half of the island's population was Christian at the time, but almost everyone took part in the mass movement.

Almost inevitably, elements alien to Christianity crept in. Cargo ideas intruded, and were mixed with the genuine Kukuaik. Graveside prayer-meetings were conducted; people believed that if they put their ears to the ground they could hear motor vehicles coming with heavy loads. Church-gatherings were also held in which everyone spontaneously began to pray together; people spoke in tongues, and there were mass seizures and foaming at the mouth. Many new songs were written and sung at this time.[4]

A man named Kubai was influential in welding cargo ideology together with Kukuaik. Kubai encouraged rumours of an imminent reversal of the existing social order. He named January 1, 1942, as the day on which the present world would end, Mount Kanigioi would topple into the sea, and a new earth would descend. Many villagers butchered pigs, fowls, and dogs, and prepared great feasts in readiness for what they called their 'Exodus' from the land of bondage. Labourers deserted the plantations and returned home to sing and dance and wait.

New Year's Day 1942 saw the arrival not of the new age, but of government officers and police from Madang. They had been summoned by exasperated and perturbed planters and missionaries. The supposed leaders of the movement were taken in custody to Madang (one of the policemen in the party was Tagarab); but on January 21 their gaol-doors were hurriedly opened as twenty-three Japanese planes bombed and strafed Madang. Kukuaik, however, was finished on Karkar.

Movements in Irian Jaya

Angganita and Others

At the same time as Letub and Kukuaik were active in the Madang area, a series of Mansren movements began in Irian Jaya.[5] In the beginning, a central figure was a Christian woman named Angganita, who is said to have recovered miraculously from death on five separate occasions. In 1939 the prophetess began to have visions; she also went into trances and spoke with different tongues. Angganita predicted the coming of Mansren Manggundi in a large, many-masted ship, bearing cargo for all. She began to rename various places: her islet became Judaea; her village, Bethlehem; and a small river nearby became Jordan. Angganita conducted rites of initiation into her movement, which grew more and more revolutionary, and attracted also educated women and men.

After Angganita was arrested and imprisoned, her place was taken by Stephanus Simopjaref, who claimed to be the new *Konoor*. Stephanus, and other leaders such as Frans and Johannes, soon incurred the wrath of the Japanese army authorities. It is thought that they, as well as Angganita, were beheaded by the Japanese in 1944.

Simson

Meanwhile, a revival of cargo expectations took place near Hollandia (now Jayapura) in Irian Jaya.[6] The leader of the movement was Simson, a Christian who claimed to have had a revelation and to be in communication with the dead. Simson's message revolved around a golden age. He announced that the messiah of Papua had prepared a great hoard of riches for the people. These treasures were not, alas, coming to the correct address because European businessmen were always altering the addresses on the crates!

Simson believed that the Papuan messiah was living in Holland, where he was busy creating all kinds of good things. His presence in the Netherlands ensured the prosperity of the colonial rulers. But soon all this would change. When the messiah returned to Irian Jaya, all foreigners would be expelled, the people would receive what was rightfully theirs, and a happy and carefree age would begin. Simson was sure that he had discovered the secret of salvation which Europeans had hitherto kept jealously to themselves. He was now about to reveal the secret to his people, so that their search for salvation could be brought to a successful conclusion.

In Papua, New Britain, New Hebrides, and Fiji

Filo

Filo, a seventeen-year-old girl, was the leading figure in a cargo movement which erupted among the Mekeo tribes at Cape Possession on the Gulf of Papua.[7] In 1941 the prophetess proclaimed herself 'queen', surrounded herself with a court of young men, and forecast the coming of a great ship which had been sent by the dead. The ship's function was to return to the people the food and other goods which had been stolen from them by the Europeans. Filo was soon supplanted as *de facto* leader of the movement by a group of men, all of whom were related to each other. These leaders persuaded the people to gather on the seashore to await the fulfilment of Filo's prophecy. As they waited, the faithful went into trances, had convulsions, and experienced collective seizures. But the ship and the cargo did not come.

John Frum

While Filo was at work in Papua, the celebrated John Frum movement was gathering momentum on Tanna in the southern New Hebrides.[8] It was believed that the god Karaperamun had appeared in a new form as 'John Frum, King of America'. At first he spoke to his people directly, but later he spoke through divine messengers known as 'ropes of John Frum'. As a result of these messages from the deity, churches were deserted, Christian villages broke up into smaller units and removed to the bush, traditional dances were renewed, and men drank *kava* once more. Many people began to spend money with reckless abandon, in the belief that the golden age would arrive only when all European money had been spent and replaced by the new currency of John Frum: a coin with a coconut stamped on it. Europeans, it was said, would leave Tanna, and then John Frum would come and give his people everything they wished for. Since the day of his coming was to be a Friday, that day replaced Sunday as the holy day. At the coming of John Frum, Tanna Island would be flattened, mountains would fill the river-beds, and the golden age would begin. John Frum would set up his own education system, sickness would vanish, and garden work would be superfluous.

The first man to proclaim himself John Frum was arrested and exposed as a fraud. His name was Manehevi, a wanderer without even a house or garden of his own. The second man, Neloiag, was committed to a home for the mentally ill. Some of the men who were active in the John Frum movement were exiled to Malekula. Despite these setbacks, faith in the coming of John Frum did not waver; sporadic outbreaks occurred throughout the 1940s. Hope is still not dead; John Frum was eagerly awaited by the majority of the population of Tanna in 1976.

Naked Cult

Some time in 1944 or 1945, a cargo movement arose among the bush communities of central Espiritu Santo in the New Hebrides.[9] This cult developed in the same general area in which the planter Clapcott had been murdered (1923) in connection with the cult led by Ronovuro. The leader of the 1945 movement was a man named Tieka (Jack). He insisted that his followers discard all their clothing, apparently in order to open the way for unrestricted sexual promiscuity. All women, including young girls, were to be readily available to any men who joined the movement. All European property was to be destroyed; all animals were to be slaughtered; no one was to work for a European. All houses were to be burned down, and two community houses were to be built. If the people followed these directions to the letter, then 'America' would come. Believers would receive cargo in abundance, and they would live for ever. To hasten this great day, a common language (Maman) was adopted, and many of the old taboos were scrapped. A road was built through the bush to the coast. Not everyone in Tieka's community was swayed by his eloquence or his promises; by 1949 even his most ardent adherents had become sceptical and disillusioned.

The 'Vessel of Christ' and Batari

In Fiji a prophet arose who called himself the 'Vessel of Christ'.[10] He promised immortality to his followers, and he boasted that he could revive the dead. This cult flourished in 1942.

About the same time, a man named Batari from Porapora, a village in New Britain, started a movement in which he organized his followers along military lines, with Batari himself as king.[11] Batari insisted that he had been informed by the spirits that all gardens were to be destroyed and all coconut trees cut down. All dogs, pigs, and fowls were to be killed and left to rot. Houses were to be pulled down, and the people were to sleep in the rain, and starve. When God saw the people suffering in this way, he would help the spirits to regain the power necessary to send to the people of New Guinea the goods which the Europeans were stealing from them.

Batari's claim that the cargo which belonged to his people was being stolen was supported by the following incident: a ship which came into port had in its hold a box marked 'battery'. Even though this box was obviously intended for Batari (since it had his name on it!), it never reached him; Europeans stole the box, and kept it and its contents for themselves. This kind of thing would not have to be tolerated much longer, for soon Batari would lead the people into a new era. Batari is said by some to have claimed to have received his commission as saviour of his people from a Czech adventurer, Zyganek, who came in a canoe to New Britain and is supposed to have said to Batari: 'Now at last I have found a man fit to be leader of his people'.[12] Batari soon came into conflict with the Japanese army authorities. He was arrested, but he survived the war and lived quietly in his village thereafter.

Cargo Movements in the New Guinea Highlands

Black King

In 1940 information which filtered down from the New Guinea Highlands indicated that cargo beliefs and expectations were not completely unknown in that region. The first Highlands cargo movement mentioned in the literature is the so-called Black King movement which occurred about 1940 near Mount Hagen.[13] Two Sepik men spread the doctrine of the original Black King movement which had been active in the Sepik and Madang districts. In the Hagen area, several clan leaders built huge warehouses in which to store the goods which the planes would bring. It was believed that previously European traders had intercepted these goods, and doled them out in niggardly fashion to the Hagen people. Soon all this would change.

The Ghost Wind

In 1943 another cargo movement, known as the Ghost Wind, began in the Markham Valley and spread to the eastern edges of the Highlands.[14] It was believed that Europeans were withholding goods which the ancestors were sending to the native people. Characteristic of this movement were outbreaks of fits and shaking (caused by the Ghost Wind), and the construction of cargo houses, inside which were placed sticks and stones and other objects. These things were expected to change into the goods which the people desired. Sometimes wooden rifles were used to drill 'soldiers'; occasionally, in fact, a government patrol was opposed by groups of men wielding these toy weapons.

Ain's Cult

Three important events preceded the outbreak of a cargo movement among the Taro people of the Enga Province.[15] In 1940-41, during the coldest winter in memory, gardens, pigs, and game were destroyed by the cold; secondly, in 1943-45 there was a severe influenza epidemic; and, thirdly, a serious disease broke out among the pigs. In 1944 the ghost of a man called Ain appeared to his four sons, informing them that the people could avert calamity by adopting new rituals. Older rituals directed to ancestral spirits were to be suspended; sacrifices were to be made to the sun by the sons of Ain who, after looking down their spear-shafts at the sun, would experience shaking fits. Ritual washing was also essential.

At first the aims of the movement appear to have been prophylactic, that is, the averting of sickness among the people and the pigs. But, as the movement spread, it collected various accretions, with the result that, in many places, there was a definite shift to an interest in the preservation of health plus the acquisition of wealth, and a further shift to a preoccupation with wealth alone. Holes were dug for pools which would be repositories for the wealth which was expected to arrive in the wake of a great darkness. After the darkness pythons would be seen hanging from the sky. Believers, it was said, would climb the pythons to the sky-world, where they would participate in the new life prepared for them, and where they would obtain the wealth which the spirits had ready for them.

Eventually, interest in Ain's Cult began to wane until it petered out entirely. Ten years after it had begun, the whole movement was regarded as a failure. Twenty years later, however, Ain's Cult was pronounced a success. Men observed that the pig herds were in better condition than before, and that a general state of well-being obtained; access to new forms of wealth had been opened up; and the millenarian preaching of some Christian missions simply confirmed the doctrine of Ain's Cult. [16]

Generally speaking, the information which is available on cargo cults in the Highlands of New Guinea is piecemeal. No coherent history exists in written form. A written history is needed, if only to give the lie to the belief that cargoism (cargo ideas and beliefs) is foreign and virtually unknown to the Highland peoples. Home-grown cults — cults not imported from other areas of Melanesia — have occurred and do occur in the Highlands. We do not know much about them simply because they have not been reported extensively in the literature.

Some Politico-Economic Movements

Toward the end of World War II several movements arose which were chiefly politico-economic in nature, but which either developed latent cargo tendencies, collected cargo accretions, or produced progeny which could be classified as regular cargo movements. Among these may be included the Tommy Kabu movement in Papua, Marching Rule in the Solomons, and the Paliau movement in the Admiralty Islands.

Tommy Kabu

Tommy Kabu was a member of the Purari I'ai clan of the Gulf Province of Papua, and the only Papuan to serve in the Australian Navy during World War II. [17] In 1946 Kabu tried to establish a number of cooperative enterprises among his people. He also set up trade links in Port Moresby which could serve as assured outlets for the cooperatives' produce. The government of the time offered Kabu a little assistance in his attempt to develop tribal lands and marketing operations, but it quickly put a stop to one other Kabu innovation: the setting up of a form of self-government in the Purari.

For various reasons, Kabu's whole project soon found itself in difficulties, and by 1956 it had virtually ground to a halt. Some of the external features of Tommy Kabu's movement were similar to certain characteristics of a cargo movement, but there is nothing to indicate that cargo thinking and cargo myths motivated the movement to a noticeable degree. Only at the end, we are told, when some people in the Purari delta saw that the movement had failed, did they begin 'to talk in cargo cult terms, but they did not actually start a cult'.[18]

Marching Rule

Post-war unrest in what was then the British Solomons became evident in the eruption of a very complex movement which had its roots in the early contact period, and which contained strong politico-nationalistic tendencies. Marching Rule, as this movement was known, began in 1944 on the island of Malaita, the most populous and, generally speaking, the least-acculturated of the Solomon Islands.[19] The two main founders of the movement, Timothy George and Nori, predicted a new social order in which everyone would be wealthy, and British rule would cease.

Marching Rule divided Malaita into nine districts, each of which was ruled over by a 'head chief', who was in turn assisted by a 'full chief'. Followers of Marching Rule were urged to refuse to pay taxes and to work on European-owned plantations. Taxes were, however, to be paid to the councils organized by Marching Rule leaders. In the movement there was a strong emphasis on the renewal of customary moral and legal values (Pidgin: *kastam*) as the guiding principles for the new society. Many people believed that Americans would come in ships to dispense goods of all kinds, and large storehouses were built to receive these goods. Thus:

> Marching Rule combined sophisticated elements of revolution, insurrection, and elemental statecraft along with completely unrealistic expectations of receiving 'cargo' and wealth as gifts, as well as deliverance from dependency status.[20]

At first, Marching Rule leaders were willing to cooperate with the Protectorate government, but soon this spirit of cooperation changed to one of opposition and passive resistance. The government responded with repressive measures; at one point two thousand passive resisters were imprisoned. Eventually, in 1952, the sentences of most prisoners were reduced or commuted, and the Marching Rule leaders agreed to the formation of a government-sponsored Malaita Council. By 1953 Marching Rule as a social movement was finished, but its ideals, hopes and aspirations lingered on, to come into focus once more in the Moro movement of 1957.

Paliau and The Noise

Paliau Maloat, who was once a First Sergeant of Police in charge of 280 men, began a movement on Manus Island in 1946-47.[21] The goals of the movement were ostensibly secular: the organizing of communal food supplies, the building up of financial resources, the cleaning and restructuring of villages, the planting of crops, and the establishing of cooperative ventures. The structure of the movement, however, was both political and religious. Paliau started what is known as the Baluan Christian Native Church, the first separatist church in Melanesia, with many rites and ceremonies borrowed from the Catholic church.

As far as can be ascertained, there was no overt cargo ritual or doctrine in Paliau's activities. But cargo ideas were injected into Paliau's movement by a man named Wapei, who began a movement known as The Noise.[22] Wapei insisted that the secular aspects of Paliau's program were wrong and unnecessary. He believed that Jesus Christ would come as the pilot of ships, manned by the ancestors, bringing all the cargo people wanted. Wapei set the following Sunday as the day for the arrival of the cargo. All work in Wapei's village ceased; everyone fasted; people prayed, sang, confessed sins, destroyed valuables, and experienced spirit-possession and convulsions. When the cargo did not arrive, Wapei corrected his mistake and named the following Sunday as the day. He also instructed his brother to kill him if the cargo did not come. The cargo did not come, so the brother split Wapei's skull with an axe.

Wapei's cult died with him, and Paliau's program absorbed the energy and hopes of those who had followed Wapei. Paliau himself, in 1947, repudiated cargo ideas, and verbally attacked the cultists. Nevertheless, the government was hostile to Paliau's innovations. In 1950 he was arrested and sentenced to six months' imprisonment for spreading false rumours. After his release, Paliau became chairman of the local government council, and was later twice elected to the national House of Assembly.

Yaliism and Related Movements

Yali

The story of Yali Singina of Sor village, on the Rai Coast about fifty miles by sea from Madang, has been told by Peter Lawrence in his magisterial work, *Road Belong Cargo*. Only the salient features of the beginnings of Yali's movement need be mentioned here. After World War II, Papua New Guinea was in turmoil. Unrest and confusion was especially serious at the village level. Because of his outstanding war record, Yali had little difficulty in securing government approval for his Rai Coast Rehabilitation Scheme, which took shape in the period 1945-48. Yali began this scheme on the assumption that the Australian administration would send cargo as a reward for war services rendered by the people. At the same time Yali believed that cargo ultimately comes from the God of the Christians, and that he would obtain it merely by an indirect route.[23]

It was almost inevitable, in an area which had a long history of cargo cultism, that Yali's rehabilitation scheme would be interpreted in terms of cargo ideology. The Mambu movement, and the myth which subsequently grew up about Mambu, provided fertile soil for a misconception of Yali's activities. But it was the Letub Cult of the early 1940s which finally perverted Yali's rehabilitation scheme into a cargo movement. Yali himself is reported to have said:

The Madangs follow me because of Letub. So they believed in me. People without Letub are not interested in me now.[24]

At first, Yali repudiated cargo doctrine, but after 1947 his attitude changed. Yali had always assumed that the Australian administration would send him and his people cargo in payment for their help during the war. So, when in 1947 he was summoned to Port Moresby, Yali expected that now at last he would be given detailed instructions regarding the receipt of the cargo. But he left Port Moresby a disillusioned man. From that point on, Yali ceased to repudiate cargo doctrine. He turned against the church and the government, and openly supported the men's cult in his village. The church, for its part, regarded Yali as an enemy; his movement was seen to be unchristian and anti-Christian. In the minds of many of his followers, Yali seems to have taken the place of the Christians' God. Some of his followers, for example, wrote a letter to one of their relatives (an evangelist), urging him to join them as disciples of Yali, and concluded their letter with the greeting: 'The grace of our Lord Yali be with you. Amen'.

In 1950 an article written for a Lutheran church-paper by the President of Lutheran Mission New Guinea acted as a catalyst for a series of actions which resulted finally in Yali's arrest and conviction on counts of illegally imprisoning people and incitement to rape.[25] During the five years which Yali spent in gaol in Lae, overt cargo activities in his name were dormant. But open support for Yali increased after his release in 1955, and especially in the 1960s. The movement which Yali had begun in 1945 continues unabated in various forms up to the present day, despite Yali's repudiation of cargo cults in 1973, and his death in 1975. The ongoing story of Yaliism will be taken up again later in this chapter.

The Komba Cult

Yali's influence was felt not only in the Madang district but also in the Morobe Province. The Komba Cult is typical of a number of movements which erupted like a rash in the wake of World War II and the Yali movement.[26] Late in 1946, a violently anti-European movement broke out among the people of Komba and Selepet villages in the mountainous hinterland of Sio. New villages were laid out in imitation of army camps, property was destroyed, and people were seized with violent fits of trembling. It was believed that the war material which had been stockpiled at the huge army-base at Finschhafen was actually intended for the local people, but the Europeans had stolen it for themselves. To prevent the rightful recipients from obtaining this material, the soldiers had dumped it in the sea when they were about to leave New Guinea. The ritual of the Komba Cult was designed not to recover this dumped cargo, but to ensure that all future cargo actually reached the people for whom it was intended. Government officers worked hard to stamp out the movement. By the middle of 1947 it had lost momentum, but the whole mountain-area inland from Sio to Finschhafen remained a hotbed of cargo cults for the next 30 years.

The *Skin Guria* Movement

In 1946-47 there broke out in the Pindiu region of the Morobe Province a cargo movement known to the local people as *skin guria* (shaking fits), and to the missionaries as the Mangzo (inner fire) movement.[27] The leaders — Botiteng from Simbeng hamlet, Anzirong from Ko village, and Iponggi from Zewezang village — had been told in a vision to go home and to await a revelation. The revelation, when it came, disclosed to them the secret of the *skin guria*. The movement which developed as a result of this revelation followed a predictable pattern. There was a great emphasis on prayers, devotions, and ritual cleanliness.

Village activities were regulated along military lines. Pigs were killed, and shaking fits were induced, as part of the leaders' attempts to contact the spirits who were expected to deliver the cargo from planes which would land in small cleared areas near the cemeteries. Moreover, cargo-laden ships and trucks would arrive from a hole in the ground which went clear through to America. Bush houses were built in which to store the expected influx of goods. There were also great expectations of revolutionary changes in the social and political order.

The *skin guria* movement, like the Komba Cult mentioned earlier, was related to and influenced by the Letub and Yali cults in the Madang area. One of the direct descendants of the *skin guria* is the Tanget Cult, which in turn gave birth to the Pitenamu Association. Of Tanget and Pitenamu we shall hear more later.

Cargo Cults on Goodenough Island

In 1946 an ex-corporal of the Pacific Islands Regiment promoted himself to the rank of sergeant, raised a white flag over his house, and announced that he was king.[28] The would-be monarch was Mwanyeta from Afufuia village on Goodenough Island. Mwanyeta appointed other men to be second-in-command and lieutenants in his army. His predictions of the imminent arrival of large ships loaded with tinned foods resulted in the neglect of garden work. People sang and danced as they waited for the cargo to arrive. However, a government officer intervened before the movement could gather momentum, and it died.

Isekele
In 1959 cargo expectations soared again as the result of the visions experienced by a ten-year-old boy named Gimaula from Wagifa Island. Gimaula was quickly replaced as guru by Isekele, an ex-preacher. He claimed to be in contact with the ancestors who had told him of the coming of a woman named Elizabeth. When she arrived by steamer the dead would arise, bringing with them the cargo which was stored underground. In order to hasten the arrival of this great day, it was necessary for believers to confess their sins, give up sorcery and adultery, and to obey the laws of the Christian church.

On August 25, 1959, one thousand followers of Isekele gathered together, for this was the day on which the cargo would arrive. But nothing happened.

Many people lost confidence in Isekele; he, however, retained sufficient faith in himself to make another attempt at a prediction concerning the coming of the cargo. On this occasion, it seems, his predictions were mixed with veiled threats against the Europeans. Isekele and two of his leading disciples were arrested, and gaoled for six months, for spreading false reports. Upon his release in May 1960, Isekele began a third movement, with the same message as before: cargo stored under Wagifa would be made accessible to the dead, who would open their graves and rejoin the living; Europeans would disappear; a new social order would be established. Isekele's spiritual authority for these predictions was the Old Testament prophet Moses. By this time, the people of Goodenough Island were not willing to lend an attentive ear to Isekele's prophecies; in many places people mocked and jeered at him. Eventually, he was arrested and imprisoned for a further six months. By the end of 1960, most people looked upon Isekele as a charlatan. His movement was dead.

The Moro Movement on Guadalcanal

A short time before Isekele began to stir up hopes on Goodenough Island, the prophet Moro initiated a movement on Guadalcanal in the Solomons, the place where a few years earlier Marching Rule had flourished.[29] In 1957, Moro, an illiterate, claimed to have been visited by a local spirit (later he said it was Jesus Christ), who told him to preach a doctrine which was a mixture of traditional values and customs, government regulations, and Christian teachings. In particular, a strong emphasis was placed on a return to traditional customs and practices (hence the name: the Moro Custom movement). There was also a definite anti-government tone, and great interest was shown in land matters. While the movement was still in its infancy, Moro was arrested and sentenced to three months' imprisonment. This served only to make Moro a minor martyr, and his movement flourished.

As the Moro Custom movement expanded, cargo beliefs spread with it. Many people said that 'black Americans' were about to send cargo, and that only the adherents of the Moro Custom would receive it. Others thought that ships from the USA would come to collect the faithful to take them back to a life of ease and luxury in the United States. In some villages, even the date was set for the arrival of the ships (August 8, 1958), and money was collected for tickets and passports.

Moro Custom was a significant social movement with political ramifications, ideologically related to the earlier Marching Rule. At its peak it exerted an influence over a large part of Guadalcanal; at its height, it probably commanded the allegiance of one-quarter to one-third of the population. Was Moro Custom a socio-nationalistic movement with accretions of cargoism, or was it essentially a cargo movement more secular and more sophisticated than its predecessors? Cargo movements of recent times are tending toward secularization in the sense that rational (from the Western viewpoint) forms of economic and social development are employed to reach traditional cargoist goals. But the powers which control the cargo still must be manipulated, and the religious duties incumbent upon those who want the cargo must still be observed.

Various Movements in Papua New Guinea in the 1960s

Ganzawa the Prophet

In 1959 a new wave of cult activity struck the Sio area of the Morobe Province.[30] The prophet Ganzawa had been making pronouncements ever since 1952, but matters came to a head in 1959 when Ganzawa predicted that at Christmas-time the earth would be transformed and the cargo would come. Many Sios living in other parts of the country returned home for the great event. There was dancing and feasting day and night. As Christmas drew near, emotions bordered on the hysterical. A few gardens were destroyed. However, a tactful intervention by the patrol officer stationed at Kalalo, coupled with the failure of anything unusual to happen on Christmas Day, brought the movement quietly and undramatically to an end — for the time being.

The Tanget Cult

The Tanget Cult was begun in the Pindiu area of the Morobe Province some time in the period 1961-64.[31] The initial impetus for the movement was provided by a series of dreams seen by Kopa Oziong from Nomaneneng village. These visions supplied information on the importance of planting the *tanget* shrub (*cordyline terminalis*), of collecting money, and of practising ritual hygiene. Traditionally, the *tanget* shrub was believed to have magico-religious powers. Its use in the Tanget Cult was to ensure the arrival of the cargo, and to emphasize indigenous identity and status over against the Europeans.

The belief system of Tanget, the procedures for collecting money, and the hygiene lessons were actively propagated by Sariong from Katken village and Akicnuc from Mindik. These leaders, however, were by no means accorded universal recognition and acceptance. They experienced strong opposition from some village elders, from administration officials, and from church leaders. Large groups of Tanget followers were placed under church discipline for extended periods. This opposition tended to confirm the cultists in their conviction that they were on the right track: the stronger the opposition, the closer they must be to the cargo secret.

The Tanget Cult is still active in the Morobe hinterland. It provides much of the ideological and ritual basis for the activities of the Pitenamu Association.

Activity in the Gulf Province

Meanwhile, among the Toaripi in the Gulf Province of Papua New Guinea, the old cargo beliefs which had been aroused by the Vailala Madness of half-a-century ago, were revived by a man named Poro.[32] He claimed that the Holy Spirit had appeared to him in a dream and instructed him to read the entire New Testament, paying particular attention to Matthew 6:4 and John 12. In subsequent dreams, Poro was commanded to hold instruction classes for his fellow-villagers. He was to tell them to keep their villages clean, to fence their burial-places, to dig a big hole in the cemetery, and to build a large community-hall. Poro did not threaten anyone or force them to join him; he simply said that people had to be part of his movement if they wanted to participate in the new way of life which was coming.

Poro's movement was one of three which were active among the Toaripi at this time. The movement started by Poro generated much discussion, and eventually it divided the community into those who were for Poro and those who opposed him. The intervention of a patrol officer helped the movement to lose momentum. People lost interest in Poro's movement, but, it is reported, Poro is

> highly regarded by many of his followers as a man deeply committed to the teachings of Christianity and as one whose prayers are a powerful aid in healing the sick.[33]

Movements in the Eastern Highlands

A cargo movement was reported in 1962 in the Upper Asaro census division of the Eastern Highlands Province.[34] The leader of the movement had had a dream in which he was instructed to go to a certain place to collect some goods which were waiting there for him. After finding the cargo, he told others about his good fortune, and persuaded them to join him in building a cargo house. Soon a fully-fledged cargo movement had evolved. People stopped work, built cargo houses, and sang and danced as they waited for the cargo. Opposition from Lutheran missionaries soon brought the movement to a halt — or so it seemed.

A similar movement occurred in the same general area in 1965, in Siokie village in the Bena Bena census division.[35] Only a few details are available. It seems that two disciples of Yali: Lagitam, and his assistant Jon Aiyovei of Sigomi village, began a movement in which people were instructed to build a large meeting-house and a smaller house in which four young girls were to live. Ritual was performed in order to attract large quantities of money. Part of the ritual was to repeat the name of Yali and then to turn the soles of the feet upward to receive the money. To ensure Yali's favourable response, about $160 were collected from Sigomi village and presented to Yali, who accepted the donation.

In 1969, at Liorofa village, a man named Nuliapo Brugue announced that ten-dollar notes were about to come floating down the Bena River.[36] He also said that cattle, sheep, and pigs would come up out of the river, so there was no need for anyone to work anymore. People stopped work, and attended meetings in an oval house every other day for three weeks. Nuliapo collected large sums of money from his people. He also gave them special instructions regarding their conduct, especially in connection with burial and other funerary rites. At dawn on the day on which the cargo was expected, most of the people from Liorofa village gathered at the river to collect the money and the cattle which would soon arrive (ovens had been prepared in which to cook the animals). However, a patrol officer who came on the scene was able to expose Nuliapo as a charlatan and a fraud; the officer was aided in this, of course, by the fact that the money and the animals did not arrive. The people demanded their money back. Nuliapo was severely beaten and forced to live in isolation for some time.

Movements on Bougainville, New Britain, and New Ireland

Longlong Lotu

Cargo activity on Bougainville Island in the 1960-1970 period could be said to have taken place on two levels.

On one level, there was traditional cargo cult activity — what is known locally as *longlong lotu*: songs and prayers to the Virgin Mary in cemeteries; magico-religious practices with the expectation that the ancestors would produce money, clothing, trucks, and other goods.[37] These activities were, and are, especially prevalent in the Bougainville hinterland. In July 1976, for example, it was reported that cultists at Kopani No. 1 village, about 50 kilometres north of Kieta, had been digging up coffins and stacking them in a house in the hope of attracting cargo.

Violence was also a feature of this movement; it was reported that some of the 500 adherents had been torturing villagers who would not join the cult.[38]

On another level, cargo beliefs and expectations found expression not in cults or cargo movements as such; rather cargo hopes focused on certain political figures, chief among whom was Paul (now Sir Paul) Lapun. It seems certain that many of those who voted for Lapun in 1964, and again in 1968, did so in the expectation that Paul Lapun would lead them along the road to cargo.[39] In similar vein, the formation of the political organization known as Napikadoe Navitu brought with it an upsurge in cargo hopes and expectations, even though the organizers of the association did their best to avert such a thing happening. Cargoism politics and business have become inextricably interwoven on Bougainville, just as they have in Madang, Lae, the Sepik, and other parts of Melanesia.

The Story Cult

Although the people of the Kaliai census subdivision of the West New Britain Province had had contact with cargo cults on a number of occasions since the Japanese invasion in 1942 (Batari's cult was probably the first), very few had actively participated in a cargo movement. In the 1960s several attempts were made to start a cargo movement, but with little success. In 1964, for example, an ex-policeman named Aikele attempted to initiate a cargo movement.[40] He announced that the people should move to Bibling Ridge where, it is said, man, coconuts, and Jesus had originated. If the people obeyed Aikele's instructions, the ancestors would send cargo in ships and planes. Aikele's people were sceptical, although some did go so far as to pay taxes to him. The government tried to make use of Aikele's leadership in the development of a copra scheme, but that failed. In the end, Aikele was rejected both by his own people and by the government.

Cargo talk which had been fostered by Aikele did not die with his abortive movement; it stayed alive and was reactivated in 1969-70 in a movement known as the Story Cult.[41] The prophet of the cult has been Na Pasisio, a 45-year-old man from Angal village, who is said to hear the voice of God and to be in direct contact with the ancestors.

Na Pasisio is searching for a road of return to the land and the ways of his forefathers. This idea is contained in the Pidgin word *stori*, a concept which plays an important part in the movement, and which gives it its name. *Stori* means myths, genealogies, and dreams or revelations. Na Pasisio has researched traditional myths and developed syncretistic ones. He has drawn up genealogies, and dreamed a number of dreams which form the ideological foundation for the movement.

According to Story ideology, cargo has been withheld from the people because the ancestors are unhappy with the wicked ways of the present generation. Accordingly, dramatic changes in life-style must be effected. People must return to the ancient sites, and live in community houses. Everything — pigs, gardens, wealth — must be shared. Everyone must learn the songs of the Story which are sung each day at dawn and at dusk to the accompaniment of confessions of wrong behaviour and selfish or angry thoughts. All this has been based on the hope that confession and singing would bring about such a high state of purity that the ancestors would be induced to send the cargo forthwith.[42]

Na Pasisio and his movement met with a mixed reception among the villagers of the Kaliai area. About half of the total population of 3,477 people participated in the movement at its peak. Those who opposed Na Pasisio were told that they would be killed by sickness, earthquakes, or tidal waves. The faithful went with the prophet on a pilgrimage to the 'place of origins' in April and May 1970. There some chosen men were shown a deep hole out of which came the sound of engines and vehicles. The spirits of the dead lived in this hole; from it would come things which would fulfil every believer's fondest hope and longing. The ancestors would come and live with the people in fine houses in a metropolis reaching from the north coast to the south coast of New Britain.

There was firm opposition to the Story on the part of the government, the missions, and some local groups. Na Pasisio was imprisoned for a short time. But the Story persists; Na Pasisio still visits his followers and urges them to 'keep the story'.

The Johnson Cult on New Ireland

At the time of the 1964 elections for the House of Assembly, a new movement emerged on the island of Lavongai in New Ireland.[43] People had been told that they could vote for whomever they fancied; so, during the elections, not a few folk voted for President Lyndon Baines Johnson of the USA. It seemed to many people that the Germans, the Japanese, and the Australians had come and gone, but very little had been done for the island. Now it was the 'time of the Americans'.

The ridicule which the 'Johnsonites' suffered because of their action in voting for the US President only served to unite them into an identifiable group. Strong anti-administration sentiment developed. People refused to pay taxes, and firm government action became necessary. Eventually, two American Catholic priests founded the Tutukuval Isukal Asosiesen (a kind of United Farmers Association), and managed to draw the people together into a developmental project which would obtain results, and which would have the approval of the government.

Various Movements in the Morobe Province

The highlands region of the Morobe Province, especially the Kabwum sub-province, was a hotbed of cargo cults in the 1960s and 1970s.[44] As we have already noted, the Tanget Cult emerged in the Pindiu area in 1962-64. The Mangzo (*skin guria*) movement continued well into the 1960s. In the Timbe area, the *luluai* of Imom began a movement in 1964 which captured the minds of large segments of the Christian community in the Ulap circuit of the Lutheran Church.[45] Typical of these various outbreaks is the one which began at Finongan in the Erap area of the Morobe Province.

The Finongan Movement
According to tradition, in a small lake near Finongan there lives a spirit called Boli.[46] Traditional stories have emphasized that if Boli were kept happy and well fed, then the people would have plenty of food in their gardens and an abundance of game in the forests.

In recent times, the story has been changed somewhat: if Boli were kept happy, the people would find plenty of money and cargo. In the lake was a radio which Boli would use to contact a man in Lae who would arrange for money and goods to be sent to Finongan. In preparation for the great day, the villages and environs, especially the cemeteries, were decorated with flowers and other things. Images of men and dogs were created out of clay, and these, too, were decorated. It was said that on the day of the coming of the cargo there would be a great darkness, accompanied by a fearful storm and an earthquake. After these phenomena had passed, a fat man would walk through the village crying: 'I believe in God the Father Almighty', but the people were to ignore him. Then a very thin man would pass through the village. He would have bright lights in his eye-sockets, and a tail light. The people were to befriend him, and to accompany him out of the village with gestures of friendship and goodwill. The thin man would be followed by a great white snake as large as a tree trunk. From this snake the cargo would pour out and fill the houses to overflowing.

This particular cargo movement flourished for about a year; it came to an end in 1969 — about the time man first set foot on the moon. The movement collapsed upon itself, without any obvious external pressures. The people of Finongan — all of them members of the Lutheran church — eventually rejected the cargo movement, and held a great service of confession, repentance, and rededication. The cargo movement was identified as a temptation from Satan.

Cargo Cults Today

Four major movements are active in their respective regions today. All wield actual or latent political power. Some of them are attempting to achieve their objectives by utilizing modern means of socio-economic development, undergirded by magico-religious 'insurance'.

Yali and the *Lo-Bos* Movement

The movement begun by Yali Singina in 1946-47 in the Southern Madang district has become institutionalized in what is called the *lo-bos* movement.[47] Even though, on April 26, 1974, Yali made an official statement dissociating himself from cargo cults, he remained nevertheless the spiritual head of the movement. After Yali's death on September 25, 1975, leadership of the *lo-bos* movement was contested by several candidates. The man most likely to wear the prophet's mantle appears to be Beig Wen, Yali's articulate secretary and close confidant. He has moved the organizational centre of *lo-bos* away from Sor and the Rai Coast to the town of Madang.

Lo in the name *lo-bos* refers to traditional rules and taboos for social behaviour. Careful observance of these rules and laws ensures a state of harmony in the community (which embraces people and spirits). If a state of 'law' is achieved, then the longed-for golden age will come. It is the function and responsibility of the *lo-bos* to look after the village *lo*.

In *lo-bos* villages, weekly meetings are held every Tuesday (Yali's birth-day). These meetings are opened with prayer to Yali, followed immediately by the confession of sins. Those who confess their sins are sprinkled with water and blessed in Yali's name. Others who have broken taboos of various kinds are fined ten toea (= cents) for each wrong. In this way an attempt is made to re-establish a state of *lo*. Baptisms which are said to undo the evil influence of Christian baptism are performed in Yali's name at a cost of two or five kina (= dollars) apiece. Another important item on the agenda for the weekly meetings is the delivering of messages which the *lo-bos* has received from Yali or from the spirit world. Political discussions also take place, touching on such topics as the millennial implications of certain political developments.

Politically, Yali's movement has allied itself with Pangu, one of three political parties active in the Madang sub-province. During the 1972 elections, one Yaliist commented:

> Pangu came. We went and saw that its policy was like the Old Man [Yali's] talk.[48]

Yali's movement, with its network of *lo-bos* and its well-organized meetings and village control, is a force to be reckoned with in the areas in which it is active. It is vigorously opposed by some local government councils and by the Christian congregations, although a few congregations seem to have worked out some sort of *modus vivendi* with the *lo-bos* movement.

The Peli Association

In 1962 a group of American surveyors erected three cement survey-markers on Mount Turu (at 4,360' the highest peak in the Prince Alexander Mountains in the East Sepik Province of Papua New Guinea).[49] These cement markers had a detrimental effect, it was said, on garden production and on the availability of game; the chief of all spirits, Wale-rur'n, who lived in the mountain, was disturbed and unhappy. Far more than trespass was involved here: Mount Turu (also called Hurun) is a sacred mountain; the presence of surveyors and their cement markers on the holy mount constituted an act of sacrilege; so the offending markers had to go. In 1969 an attempt was made to remove one of the markers, as a result of which the two leaders, Mathias Yaliwan and Daniel Hawina, were gaoled. But the problem of the cement markers remained.

After his release from gaol, Mathias Yaliwan, the prophet and spiritual head of the movement which had developed, predicted that on the seventh day of the seventh month, after the offending markers had been removed, game would once more become plentiful, gardens would flourish, and political self-government and independence would be attained. People from the East and West Sepik region, and from places as far away as Lae and Port Moresby, fought to become financial members of Yaliwan's movement. By 1971 the amount of $21,572 was held in two boxes in Daniel Hawina's place.

Expectations about what would happen on July 7, 1971, far exceeded the announced or 'official' expectations. It was thought, variously, that there would be a long night during which people would turn white, and all dogs, pigs, birds, and other animals would return to their place of origins. During this long night, people would be visited by snakes and reptiles and a huge python. When the long night was finished, Europeans and natives would sit down and eat together. Some people said that a huge wave would swamp the Prince Alexander Mountains; others thought that there would be a great fog and earthquakes, followed by a sickness which would sweep the land. Other people believed that 300 American 707 jet aircraft would land on the mountain-top and disgorge friendly Americans, money, and cargo.

July 7, 1971, came and went; apart from the ceremonial removal of the cement markers, nothing happened. A few days later the Peli Association was formed with membership fees of ten or twelve kina. Initially, there was a great deal of ritual activity directed toward the attempt to find the *rot bilong mani* (the way to money). Memorial plots were sold in the expectation that they would produce money, but this scheme was soon abandoned. Another activity which was performed on Monday, Wednesday, and Friday nights was the sifting of money from one dish to another by girls called 'flowers'. This was a difficult activity, but it did (so it is said) produce money. Eventually, this ritual activity also ceased.

Another activity which was undertaken with great enthusiasm was the carrying of red suitcases. A man would purchase a red wooden suitcase, similar to those used by priests throughout the district to carry the elements for the Mass. He would then pay Daniel Hawina a fee (up to 100 kina), leave the case in Hawina's house for a time, collect it later from Hawina, and carry it carefully home. This act of carrying home the suitcase was loaded with almost impossible taboos.

> Some said the carrier of the box had to be a virgin, or at least to have abstained from sex for some time. The box was to be carried in absolute silence, whatever the distance home. It was to be held before you, resting on your arms; and the carrier should look neither to right nor left.[50]

With so many taboos involved, no one could be really surprised, when he reached home and opened the suitcase, to find only stones, or lime, or his own money.

The Peli Association has not yet developed into an effective business organization, even though it is has had quite large sums of money at its disposal (estimates range from K100,000 to K200,000). Nor has Peli emerged as a powerful political force, even though Yaliwan was elected to the House of Assembly in 1972, and his successor in 1974 was a member of the Peli Association. Undoubtedly, certain political hopes and longings centre on the person of Mathias Yaliwan. In August 1976, Linus Hepau, Yaliwan's successor in parliament, announced that he had been instructed by people in his electorate to inform the country that Yaliwan should be appointed Head of Papua New Guinea, and that Yaliwan's likeness should appear on the coins of Papua New Guinea.

Mathias Yaliwan has broken with the Peli Association and formed a new organization called the Seven Association. Daniel Hawina insists, however, that Yaliwan is still the spiritual head of the Peli Association.

John Frum

The island of Tanna in the New Hebrides has a population of 12,000, the majority of whom are waiting for the arrival of John Frum, the local messiah who is coming from America to inaugurate the golden age.[51] The hope is expressed that the American GIs will be lured back to Tanna, bringing with them the cargo-laden Liberty ships. To this end, marching men with the letters U S A emblazoned on their chests hold mock military drills with rifles made of bamboo. Fifty thousand soldiers are believed to have gathered beneath the island's smoking volcano, waiting for the day of John Frum's coming. To hasten that day, the faithful place flowers on red John Frum crosses, and spend much time in prayer and meditation before the crosses.

Some people believe that the changing cultural patterns on Tanna have made John Frum angry. Hence, even though aircraft continue to be used to shift Tanna produce, there is a strong move to reintroduce traditional dress and ritual. Magic is practised openly, as is also the drinking of *kava*. In general, the islanders are loath to cooperate with the New Hebridean authorities lest they compromise their fidelity to John Frum.

Pitenamu

Pitenamu as a movement began in the Pindiu area of the Morobe Province.[52] The name 'Pitenamu' is an acronym derived from the first two letters of the four regions from which the association initially derived support: Pi = Pindiu; Te = Tewae; Na = Nawae; Mu = Mumeng. Pitenamu is an attempt on the part of the people themselves to do something about the lack of development in the mountain areas of the Morobe Province. At first, the society was loosely organized: the collecting and receipting of membership-fees took place rather haphazardly. The government welfare officer tried to regularize the society's affairs by insisting that only duly-appointed men be authorized to collect moneys; that receipts be given for all funds collected; and that the society be guided in its economic operations by a qualified adviser.

In October 1974, Pitenamu purchased 7,000 $1.42 shares in the transport company, Pagini Brambles Transport Pty Ltd, with an option to buy 15 per cent of shares in the company. Earlier, the society had operated several passenger vehicles and trade stores. The regularizing of the society's affairs continued when Mr Boyamo Sali, the then Minister for State, presented membership cards to financial members on July 26, 1975.

The various activities of Pitenamu are undergirded by magico-religious ritual in order to ensure their success. It is probable that these rituals make it easy for less-sophisticated people to have the same expectations from Pitenamu as they have from cargo cults. A leading figure in Pitenamu is Nubos Jengenu from Zewezang village. He was a disciple of Sariong, and had dealings with Akicnuc and Kopa of Tanget Cult fame. It is possible that Nubos and other officers of Pitenamu have been able to work out an accommodation between cargo thinking and business action; but many followers in distant villages see Pitenamu only as a variation on the cargo cult theme.

In its present form, Pitenamu may be described as a venture into economic, political, and social development by a cooperative which has not broken completely from its moorings in cargoism. The ideological roots of Pitenamu are to be found in the *skin guria* movement of the 1940s. A development of that movement was the Tanget Cult. One of the progeny of Tanget is Pitenamu.

Pitenamu is not yet an economic or political force in the Morobe Province. It has allied itself with the political party Pangu in the sense that there is a significant overlap in membership of Pangu and Pitenamu. But there is no formal alliance. Whether there will be one in the future seems to depend, on the one hand, on whether Pangu can revitalize the tottering party-structure in the Province, and, on the other hand, on whether Pitenamu can survive and flourish in the world of business with its fluctuations in share values and its calls for further capital, and still retain its appeal to the people in the hinterland of the Morobe Province.

More than money is invested in Pitenamu. Men and women have come to look upon it as the means by which their hopes and longings and expectations and dreams will be fulfilled. Pitenamu represents hope for the future, an opportunity to regain one's pride and self-respect. It is, as one ardent supporter of Pitenamu said to a tertiary student:

> One day you will become a worker in my company, because I am trying to find a way out for myself and you are not. Now is the time to experiment with various ways of finding the road to future success and happiness. Your teachers are not helping you to find the way for yourself. I'm sorry for you. I am a member of Pitenamu, and today, tonight, tomorrow the good life will be mine.

Chapter 3

THE PROBLEM OF INTERPRETATION

Cargo cults have many faces. They are, therefore, the despair of theorists who try to fit them into predetermined social, anthropological, political, or theological patterns. Kenelm Burridge, who has written several outstanding monographs on cargo movements, was not merely being facetious when he wrote in a book review:

> Cargo cults might be very like omnivorous but servile chameleons. They gobble up positivist and mechanistic social theory and have plenty of spit left over; they are very good at appearing as any one might imagine them to be. Platonists, football-poolers, situational-logickers — they can all have a go.[1]

Many men and women have, indeed, 'had a go' at interpreting cargo cults. Their efforts are surveyed in this chapter.

What Are Cargo Cults?

Cargo cults are more easily described than defined or interpreted. A classical cargo movement usually begins with an announcement by a prophet or leader that he has had a dream or vision which has revealed to him information about the imminent return of the ancestor or ancestors. The message predicts that the arrival of the ancestors will be preceded by clear signs, often cataclysmic in nature. An earthquake or flood may be predicted; perhaps there will be a volcanic eruption or a tidal wave, or signs will appear in the sun and moon, or a great darkness will cover the earth before a new cosmic structure emerges.

After the prophet has made his announcement and predictions, the villagers usually follow him in a series of actions: all ordinary work comes to an abrupt halt; pigs and chickens are slaughtered in a holocaust; savings are spent or thrown away; property and harvests are destroyed — all with the idea of hastening the arrival of the spirits of the dead with the cargo they will bring. Sometimes huge warehouses are built to accommodate the new goods which are expected in abundance. Finally, graves are cleaned and preparations are made for feasts at which the returning dead will sit down and eat with the living.

There is often a strong emphasis on cleanliness, ritual purification, and adherence to strict moral injunctions. The few instances in which sexual licence is an integral part of the cargo ritual are outnumbered by the majority of cases in which strong taboos are directed against sexual excesses or irregularities both within and outside the marriage relationship.

If, after all the activity and preparations, the ancestors do not come at the time expected, then more action becomes necessary. A mass hysteria often takes hold. Quaking and shaking, glossolalia, visions and dreams are experienced. The prophet or leader will sometimes modify or change his initial predictions, or he will order changes in the rituals of preparation. For example, if part of the preparations has involved the complete rejection of all things European, the leader might reverse the instructions to the effect that his followers must embrace to the fullest extent the clothing, manners, and religious beliefs of the European. Eventually, people realize that the cargo and the new age are still not within their grasp, and enthusiasm wanes. Life more or less returns to normal until another prophet arises and the whole cycle is repeated.

These, then, are the external features of a typical cargo movement. Obviously, no one movement will contain all the features mentioned, for there are countless variations on the theme. Guiart and Worsley have identified nine components which they consider to be characteristic of conventional cargo movements.[2] These features are:

1) the myth of the return of the dead;
2) a revival or modification of paganism;
3) Christian elements;
4) belief in the cargo myth;
5) belief that the Melanesians will become white men, and vice versa;
6) belief in the coming of a messiah;
7) attempts to restore native economic and political control;
8) violence or threat of violence against whites;
9) unification of traditionally separate and hostile groups.

The most common factor is belief in the cargo myth. The specific elements of the myths which undergird cargo cults are discussed later in this chapter. By way of anticipation, we may note that the cargo myth or the myths which establish the 'cargo ambience' (Burridge) have a plot-line which is almost predictable in its regularity: in the hoary past, our ancestors made a choice or performed an action which was to their detriment. That is why we are in our present predicament. But our ancestors have learnt the right way, and they will soon share it with us.

The least-common characteristic of a cargo movement is belief in the coming of an individual messiah. But this characteristic would be given a high ranking if the messiah were thought of as a collective figure, that is, the ancestors as a group.

A tenth characteristic might well have been added to the nine in Guiart and Worsley's list:

10) a phoenix-like tendency to revive after apparent failure and death.

The history of cargo cults is the history of a succession of movements which appear to have failed. Yet, cargo cults and cargo beliefs persist. It seems that, even though a specific cargo movement meets with no apparent success, the cargo myths or the cargo ideology are in no way invalidated. People will look for the causes of failure in themselves or in external influences, but the basic cargo beliefs are rarely challenged.

Frustrations for the Interpreter

A review of the short history of the interpretation of cargo cults in Melanesia shows that, although interpretations in great number and variety have been offered, no single explanation has met with general approval.[3] This lack of unanimity among the students of cargo cults is reflected in the diversity of names by which the movements are designated. Some of the names which theoreticians will defend quite vehemently are: cargo cults or movements; messianic movements; millenarian movements; nativistic movements; adjustment movements; revitalistic movements; nationalistic movements; commodity millennialism; and several others.

The *what* of cargo cults is closely related to the *why* question: why do cargo cults occur in some areas and not in others, and why do more occur in some areas than in others? A wide variety of answers has been given to the *why* question. Outbreaks of cargo cults have been attributed to the presence or absence of economic development; the presence or absence of Christian missions; the presence or absence of educational and other alien social institutions; or, simply, to the presence or absence of Americans, Japanese, Russians, and so on. Within these general categories, there are further sub-divisions. Protestants, for example, might suggest that cargo cults are more prolific in Catholic areas than they are in Protestant areas. Or, mainline Protestant churches will maintain that the sects are cargo-cult catalysts: Jehovah's Witnesses and Seventh Day Adventists are the scapegoats. And, even in a single denomination such as the Lutheran Church, a minor war of words has been waged over the question of why cargo cults have broken out in the area served by one group of missionaries and not in an area served by a different group.

One of the major problems in the matter of interpretation is that the conclusions to which an interpreter comes are often controlled by, and dependent upon, the interpreter's own presuppositions and methodology. In effect, the interpretation which is proposed is simply a working out of the interpreter's own preconceived notions about the movements.

The *basic* problem, however, seems to be that published interpretations have heretofore been offered only by Europeans, that is, by non-Melanesians. Western observers have attempted to interpret a non-Western cultural and religious phenomenon on the basis of their own Western epistemology (and, obviously, any interpretation offered in this book suffers from just that short-coming).

The dilemma is plain and acute: cargo cults are too prolific and too important to be ignored; an effort must be made to understand them on their own terms. But, up to now, the only interpreters who have committed their thoughts to the printed page are non-participating foreigners who bring to their task a host of alien intellectual, moral, religious, political, and social values and presuppositions. Fortunately, an end to the dilemma appears to be in sight. Non-Melanesians should not have to wait much longer before a Melanesian articulates for them in detail his understanding of what cargo cults are all about.

Five Categories of Interpretation

The interpretations of cargo cults which have been advanced during the past 50 years or so may be placed into five broad categories. The borderline between the various kinds of interpretation cannot always be drawn with precision; the groupings, however, might be useful for purposes of review and for obtaining an overall picture of the range of interpretations which have been proposed.

The five categories suggested by Steinbauer are as good as any. They are: 1) the socio-political; 2) the Christian-ethical; 3) the cultural-historical; 4) the national-economic; and 5) the eclectic. [4]

The Socio-Political Interpretation

Proponents of the socio-political interpretation believe that cargo cults occur because the affected society lacks sufficient 'cultural insurance' to withstand the shock of sudden contact with another culture. As a consequence, the society finds itself in a state of frustration and stress. In many cases this condition is brought about by contact with Western culture. The Melanesian movements are to be interpreted as defensive mechanisms which ensure, on the one hand, that the traditional cultures do not appear poor in comparison with the alien one, and, on the other hand, that provision is made for the obtaining of the desirable elements in the new culture.

Vittorio Lanternari is a representative of the socio-political group of interpreters.[5] Lanternari finds that the cargo cults of Melanesia are 'a religious reflection of the sharp cultural antagonism' between Western and Melanesian civilization. The arrival of Western goods and technology constitutes the moment of impact between two types of civilization which have inevitably taken different courses. The people of Melanesia react to the encounter between indigenous and Western techniques by resorting to a mythical interpretation: Western material goods and technology are of supernatural origin. We Melanesians have always believed that the dead will return to earth, endowed with supernatural powers to bring unheard-of riches to the living. The new goods must be these riches. They are brought by the Europeans, to whom belongs the mantle of magic which traditionally belonged to the returning dead. Lanternari concludes:

> The nativistic movements reveal that the point of exhaustion has been reached by the traditional religion in its effort to procure salvation (salvation being the purpose of all religion); and by imparting new impulses to spiritual life in the masses they are able to meet the challenge of renovation thrown up by the drastic experiences to which their society has been subjected.[6]

The Christian-Ethical Interpretation

A recent representative of the Christian-ethical interpretation is Hermann Strauss.[7] Strauss, a missionary-anthropologist, thinks that the Melanesian movements are the outward expression of a burning inner desire for a full, complete life. The Melanesian hopes for a golden age. He hopes for salvation and peace, for a long and happy life now and hereafter. His chief question is: How may my longings for a complete life be met here and now? The answer he gives is that, somehow, the powers of this world must be so manipulated as to reveal the way to the source of all spiritual and material blessings.

Strauss notes that this conclusion must be examined in the light of the peculiar Melanesian cosmology. Many Melanesians believe that heaven, earth, and the underworld are filled with mysterious powers of salvation or destruction. These powers can be controlled by *shamans*, prophets, witchdoctors, or messiahs. The arrival of the Europeans, with all their goods, knowledge, and 'supernatural' powers, convinced many Melanesians that in Western culture and religion lies the secret of the way to all blessings. The Melanesians, Strauss says, could not be sure that the ancestors, the benevolent spirits and the supernatural powers of traditional religions, were strong enough to bring about the longed-for golden age. So, men turned to the God of the Christians. It was believed, for example, that the *parousia* of Christ would usher in the golden age for which men had hitherto waited in vain.

Strauss sees cargo cults, in their present form, as a mixture of traditional and Christian beliefs in the coming age of wholeness, health, healing, and material and spiritual blessings. He interprets the ideology of the movements as a distortion of the biblical view of man. Scripture confesses that God is the centre of all existence. Cargo cults tend to put man in the place of God. The praise, honour, and glory which is due to God is given to man. But, Strauss concludes, the 'most blasphemous' aspect of the cargo ideology is the utter perversion of the meaning and purpose of the death of Christ. Christ is no longer the 'author and finisher of the faith', but the initiator of a higher and better culture.

The Cultural-Historical Interpretation

The third group of interpreters is composed largely of ethnologists and anthropologists. Palle Christiansen may be cited as one representative of this group.[8] He believes that:

> it is in the internal social structure that we should look for the conflicts which start off the process of cultural and social change.

In times of crisis, men try to find answers out of their own mythical heritage, and, by so doing, they hope to control the present. Thus, the key for reaching an understanding of the movements is to be found in traditional beliefs, ritual, and mythology.

Another representative of the cultural-historical type of interpretation is Mircea Eliade.[9] His approach is somewhat speculative, but nonetheless suggestive of the possible direction in which one might go for a satisfactory accounting of all the available data. Eliade sees the cargo movements in Melanesia as an extension of a fundamental religious notion which appears everywhere in the region, that is, the myth of the annual return of the spirits of the dead and the renewal of the cosmos. The cosmos must be renewed annually, and at the new year festivals, where the regeneration of the cosmos is accomplished, the dead are present. This idea is further extended and elaborated in the myth of the Great Year, in which a total renewal of the cosmos is brought about by the complete destruction of existing forms. This return to chaos is followed by a new creation, which is modelled on the original creation. Eliade proposes that the cargo cults have simply taken over a traditional theme, enriched it, charged it with new values, and given it prophetic and millenarian content.

Eliade suggests that in the Christian religion the Melanesians thought that they had discovered their old traditional eschatological myths. But, he charges, these very eschatological and prophetic aspects of Christianity were not taken seriously by Christian missionaries. The Melanesians thought that the missionaries were unwilling to preach and practise true Christianity, because by so doing they would reveal the key which opens the door to the new age.

The National-Economic Interpretation

The national-economic type of interpretation is championed, in the main, by sociologists and ethnologists writing after World War II. Peter Worsley is an able representative of this group.[10] Worsley interprets the cargo movements as a reaction to the oppression exercised by foreign powers. The people of Melanesia were formerly divided into small, separate, and isolated social groups: the village, the clan, the tribe, the people of the valley. They lacked centralized political institutions and, therefore, had no apparatus for acting as a united force in political matters. They had no legal machinery apart from the counsel of the elders, or of people who had acquired prestige by the accumulation of wealth or by fighting prowess.

A low level of political organization is typical, Worsley believes, of societies among which there is a certain 'predisposition' toward millenarian movements such as cargo cults. Other factors which contribute to the establishment of a climate favourable to cargo cults are centred around the society's lack of technological and scientific knowledge. The people are quite ignorant of the findings of modern science on the origins and causes of various diseases, on animal husbandry, on variations in soil fertility, on changes in climate, on the movements of the planets, and so forth. These deficiencies in scientific knowledge and practice leave the field wide open to interpretations and explanations in terms of supernaturalism and animism. People are, thus:

> predisposed to the acceptance of supernaturalist interpretations of reality: the soil is tilled for the millenarian leader. As pragmatic social experience increases and as education spreads, the ground becomes less fertile for millenarianism.[11]

Worsley makes no secret of his attempt to interpret the Melanesian movements in harmony with Marxist theory. The movements are 'pre-political'. Their effect is to fuse a divided, suppressed, and exploited population into an active political unit. Thus, the movements provide the integration which is necessary if the community wishes to satisfy newly-arisen needs. The real problem, however, is that the only possibility of common action which the traditional Melanesian system offers is on the magico-religious plane. All other alternatives which might enable the Melanesian to compete with Europeans are nullified by the latter's apparent superiority.

Eclectic Interpretations

A large number of interpreters seek to occupy middle ground between extreme positions. They see themselves as neutral observers, interested chiefly in trying to fit together the various pieces in the interpretative puzzle in an effort to gain a composite picture of the movements.

Typical of this group is Friedrich Steinbauer. [12] He believes that contact with Western civilization is a primary cause of cargo cults. There are, however, a number of factors within the Melanesian cultures themselves which also contribute to the rise and spread of cargo cults. Some of these cultural factors are: magical thinking, in which rituals of analogy are thought of as powerful means of achieving desirable goals; eschatological hopes which are based on mythological forms; a concept of time which conflicts with a Western historical outlook (there is a future, but that future is not thought of as moving toward a definite end or goal); a keen desire for material possessions; climatic conditions which tend to affect mental reactions; and certain psychic structures which create a tendency to fantasy.

Steinbauer suggests that the cargo cults of Melanesia should be regarded as expressions of legitimate human hopes and desires. They are honest, but misguided, attempts to achieve a happy and useful human existence. Their goal is 'salvation', which is seen in the totality of life: there is no separation of spiritual salvation (= German *Heil*) from physical salvation (= German *Wohl*). Cargo cults hold out hope for Melanesians, even for Christian Melanesians. Why do they cling to such hope? Steinbauer replies:

> The answer is easy: Because they too remain Melanesians and cannot simply bypass or invalidate certain categories of thought or experience. Even more so because Melanesians — like people the world over — can remain human only if they go on hoping, go on transcending their experience, go on seeking to cross the boundaries of the given and to comprehend salvation as the foundation of life. [13]

Areas of Consensus

One conclusion which may be drawn from the preceding review of the interpretations of cargo cults is that the problem of explanation still awaits a definitive solution. On some points, one interpretation appears to contradict another; on other points, the interpretations are not contradictory, but they are clearly divergent. Those who know something about cargo cults will probably find one or two ideas with which they can agree in each of the proposed interpretative approaches.

Interpreters appear to have arrived at a consensus on several issues. One area concerns the explanation for the spread of the movements among widely-separated groups. It is generally agreed (although there are some notable dissenters) that this spread cannot be explained in terms of normal cultural diffusion, that is, geographical transmission by contagion. This is, of course, a negative consensus, but it is a consensus.

Another area — an important area — in which there is growing agreement concerns the starting-point for an understanding of cargo cults. More and more interpreters are coming to the conviction that cargo cults and cargo beliefs are not alien imports into the Melanesian religious system. They are, rather, an integral part of that system, and they give expression to some of the deepest Melanesian religious hopes, beliefs, and aspirations. Thus, Dorothy Counts, for example, in her discussion of why the Kaliai people were attracted to the Story Cult, concludes that:

[The Story] did not violate fundamental beliefs. Cargo belief, whether or not it is at any given time expressed in an organized systematic cargo movement, is consistent with the concept of reality. Joining the Story required no fundamental leap of faith or conversion to a new religious system.[14]

This realization, that cargo ideology constitutes part of the fundamental data of religious beliefs in Melanesia, constitutes a major breakthrough in the Western understanding of cargo cults. A corollary of this insight is another: no interpretation of cargo cults is valid which does not take into account the basic role which myths play in the movements.

Myth in Melanesia

In his book *Myth and Ritual in the Old Testament*, Brevard Childs defines myth as:

a form by which existing structures of reality are understood and maintained.[15]

Child's definition is only occasionally true with reference to the function of myth in Melanesia.

In some instances it can be demonstrated that myths do serve to preserve existing structures in the society. In many other cases, however, it is clear that the myth is regarded as the dynamic for introducing radical changes in the social structures. The validity, integrity, and power of a myth is not dependent upon the success or failure of the movement which has drawn life from the myth. Even when the myth has been the enabling force behind a movement which apparently fails to meet its objectives, confidence in the myth is not shaken. The myth is constantly updated, revised, modernized, and made relevant to the existential situation. It may even be reinterpreted. But, as Burridge and Lawrence have demonstrated,[16] the essential core and character of the myth remains.

Vis-a-vis religious movements in Melanesia, myth may be said to exercise a threefold function. First, myth may be employed to justify changes which are expected or proposed. Secondly, myth may provide the incentive or the dynamic for movement toward change and renewal in the society. Thirdly, myth may supply the model or the blueprint for the change which is awaited.

This last function of serving as a model is especially important. According to the cyclical view which Melanesians appear to have of time and history, the future is in some way a replay of the past. In a very real sense there is 'nothing new under the sun', as the ancient Preacher said. In the myth the past is preserved — yes, in a stylized and perhaps idealized form — but preserved to serve as a model for the events of today and the hopes of tomorrow. Mircea Eliade once described myth as 'exemplar history'.[17] This description would constitute a major part of the definition of the function of myth in Melanesia.

Basic Themes in Melanesian Mythology

The myths which undergird the Melanesian cargo cults vary greatly in matters of detail. Yet, it is possible to identify five themes which occur consistently.[18]

The first theme is that of the division of mankind. In the myth, a situation is presented in which a choice is made, and this choice serves to divide one progenitor from another, one group of descendants from another group. Typical is this myth from the people of Tangu:

> A certain woman had no husband to protect her. One day she left her daughter alone and a stranger came and killed the child and buried the body. The woman learned the whereabouts of the grave in a dream. She recovered the body, and, carrying it in her string bag, she wandered from village to village until she found a place to bury her child, and a man, the younger of two brothers, who would marry her. She had two sons by her new husband [the sons were named Tuman and Ambwerk].

By and by she visited the daughter's grave. Parting some coconut fronds she found salt water flowing from the grave, and fish swimming. The woman took some water and a small fish as food for her family. The results were miraculous. Overnight her son grew to manhood. Her husband's elder brother was envious and wanted the same for his son, so she directed him to the grave. Instead of taking a small fish the foolish man seized a large eel-like one. Immediately the ground quaked and water thundered forth from underground, forming the sea and separating brother from brother. After a while the two brothers re-established contact by floating messages to each other written on leaves. It soon became apparent that the younger brother was able to invent and make wonderful things like boats with engines, umbrellas, rifles, and canned food while the elder brother could only make copies.[19]

The theme of the two brothers is the second common motif. This must, surely, be one of the most-widespread mythological themes in Melanesia. The myth usually tells of an act of hostility or stupidity by one of the brothers, an act which causes the two to go their separate ways. The hope is expressed that there will be a reconciliation, which will also restore the world and society to its pristine good order. The Manup-Kilibob myth, with its many variations, is a good example of this kind of myth-motif.[20]

A third theme is that of a lost Paradise. The myth tells of how a once-idyllic existence was spoilt by foolishness, disobedience, or ingratitude on the part of an individual or a group. The Mansren myth from Irian Jaya is typical.[21] The Tolai of New Britain have a number of legends which tell of how death came into the world as a result of man's disobedience. For example:

The old woman died, but she lived again. She called her two sons, To Kabinana and To Purgo, and said, 'Bring fire'.
But To Purgo said, 'There is no fire'. For he thought to himself that the woman was really dead.
The old woman said, 'If you had done what I told you and brought me fire, you would have lived for ever. Because you did not fulfil my wish and bring me fire to warm myself and keep you alive for ever, you will die as I do.'[22]

The coming of the end-time is a fourth theme. The description of the *eschaton* often resembles some of the descriptive passages in Jewish apocalyptic literature. The cosmic upheaval which is predicted is thought of as a prelude to the arrival of the messiah-figure.[23]

The advent of the messiah or saviour-hero is the fifth common motif in Melanesian myths. The expected deliverer is often 'some historical figure invested with a religious aura'. He will return, and many ancestors will return with him. The dead will sit with the living at an eternal banquet. The golden age will begin. This age 'may represent a folk-memory of an actual earlier epoch in the society's history, however idealized'.[24]

In connection with this fifth theme of the coming of the ancestors to earth, it is worthwhile noting a difference which exists in the beliefs of people within Melanesia itself. In some parts of the Highlands of Papua New Guinea (for example, in the Enga Province), the last thing the people would want is for the ancestors to come to earth. To be told that the ancestors are about to return is to receive a threat, not a promise. Hence, for the Enga, the desirable goal is not one which involves the return of the ancestors, but one which requires those living on earth to make their way to the place of the sky people. [25]

'Religions of Return' and the Search for Salvation

We have seen that, in order to give explanations for present conditions, and to express hopes for an improved future situation, the myths reach back to what is believed to be the origins of the world and society. Cargo ideology, which is based on these myths, draws on its understanding of how things were in the pristine past in order to make sense of present realities and to give hope for the future. This tendency to return to the origins of the society is so marked in all messianic and millenarian movements throughout the world that Vittorio Lanternari has suggested that the movements be called 'religions of return'. Lanternari's studies lead him to the conclusion:

> the religion of return is the essential kernel of messianism as such. Through it the era of salvation appears mythically as the reinstatement of the age of origins. [26]

All these 'religions of return' — including the Melanesian cargo cults — have as their goal 'salvation'.

All these religions are searching for salvation. The salvation which is sought resembles in many ways the kind of salvation the poets of the Old Testament described: a salvation rooted in concrete experiences and situations. For the psalmists, salvation meant deliverance from deadly danger, healing in sickness, liberation from captivity, ransom from slavery, help in a lawsuit, victory in battle, peace after political negotiations, and so forth. [27] Salvation was now, this-worldly, to do with everyday life; it was not especially 'spiritual'. Salvation in the sense of being saved from sin does not receive a major emphasis in the Old Testament. [28]

The salvation which is sought in the 'religions of return' embraces such things as deliverance from present troubles and oppression, peace, wholeness, healing, health and well-being. This salvation will be achieved, so it is believed, when the ideal models for man's behaviour and his social institutions which were established in the historical or mythical past are actualized and restored in the present age.

Cargo cults may be understood as the Melanesian version of the search for salvation. Having advanced that theological proposition, we immediately run into a difficulty — one created not by cargo cults, but by theology.

Traditional Christian theology has been unwilling to admit that the concept 'salvation' may legitimately be used in connection with non-Christian religions. Christian theology sees salvation not as a general category, but as a unique one.[29] Salvation comes to man only as a consequence of God's gracious activity in Christ Jesus (Tit. 2:11-12), proclaimed to men in the Gospel of Jesus Christ (2 Cor. 5:18 - 6:2 However, does not Christianity's insistence on the universality of God's salvation (John 3:16; 1 Tim. 2:3-7) imply also a universal need? And does not the Bible insist that all men are in need of salvation (Rom. 1:18 - 3:20)? It should come as no surprise, then, to find that men the world over are searching for salvation. In fact, as a recent Vatican publication stated:

> The search for salvation is recorded in the very dynamism of the human mind, indeed it appears as the fundamental and the universal aspect of it . . . Whatever else a religion may or may not be, it is essentially a reaching forward to the ideal of salvation.[30]

The recognition that many religious movements in the world are, in essence, a search for salvation is not in itself a denial of the uniqueness of Christ and of Christian salvation. The two basic questions which Christian theology puts to any religionist are: To whom do you look for your salvation? and, How is your salvation achieved? In suggesting that the Melanesian cargo cults may be viewed theologically as a search for salvation, we are not implying that the cargo cults are a road to salvation parallel to the Christian way, or even that the Melanesian search for salvation is a legitimate one. Cargo cults, too, have to answer the two fundamental questions concerning the *who* and the *how* of salvation.

By identifying cargo cults as a search for salvation, we are seeking to remove the debate from the field of anthropology or sociology or psychiatry or political theory, and to transfer it to the religious forum. If cargo cults are, in fact, religious movements, here is where the discussion finally belongs.

From here we may move in several directions. We may follow the lead of Lanternari, Eliade, and Turner,[31] for example, and undertake a study of cargo cults as part of the phenomenology of religions. Or, we may attempt to take a specifically-theological look at cargo cults, reflecting upon them in terms of basic themes in Christian theology. Either way will bring us to a better understanding of cargo cults, and will uncover for us the extent of the challenge which Christianity confronts in cargoism.

Chapter 4

CARGO CULTS IN THEOLOGICAL PERSPECTIVE

No one, who has surveyed the rich biblical resources available to those who want to do a theology of cargo cults, could fairly accuse the Holy Spirit of being a niggard or a miser. God has, in fact, been so generous that the would-be interpreter of cargo cults has something of a problem deciding what to do with all the biblical concepts, motifs, and themes which lay claim to relevance in any theological discussion of cargo cults.

The interpreter has several options before him. He may, if he wishes, cast his net wide, and attempt to do justice to every relevant theme and motif of biblical theology. By so doing, he runs the risk of producing vague generalizations and bland syntheses which distort and caricature biblical theology instead of faithfully reflecting the diversity within its intrinsic unity. Or he may elect to pick and choose from the various biblical themes and concepts, judiciously selecting those which seem most suitable for his purposes. He thereby gets to have reasonable control of his material, but leaves himself open to the suspicion that he is manipulating biblical theology to fit his own understanding of what cargo cults are and are not.

Perhaps a compromise promises the best solution. That is, in making eclectic use of the biblical material, we try to choose that which has a kind of built-on or innate cohesiveness. The Old Testament, for example, is an identifiable unit which appears to be particularly relevant to the Melanesian situation. Many of the cultural, social, and religious patterns of the Old Testament communities find an echo in Melanesia. Several Old Testament themes or motifs could very well provide the basis and the stimulus for fruitful theological reflection upon cargo cults.

But even more suitable for the purposes of our study is the body of material known as the Pauline *corpus*, the writings of the Apostle Paul.[1] The apostle makes constant and creative use of the Old Testament and of the literature from the inter-testamental period; ideas, themes, motifs, concepts, and presuppositions from there fill his epistles. But, writing as he does on this side of the Resurrection, Paul has reshaped, reworked, and reinterpreted old themes and notions, and given them new life and new meaning. He has corrected misconceptions which had arisen, and given the lie to falsehoods and heresies which had crept into Judaism's reading and understanding of the Old Testament. In Pauline theology we have the inspired results of apostolic reflection upon key Old Testament themes.

Another reason for concentrating on the theology of the Apostle Paul is that Paul was a man of two worlds. He was a Jew, a trained rabbi, steeped in the Old Testament and in rabbinic lore. He was very conscious of his people's history, of their hopes, beliefs, and expectations. Messianism and apocalypticism were his bread and butter. He knew the temper of the times — times which, in some respects, were remarkably similar to the situation which has prevailed in Melanesia during the past century. In Paul's day, people expected the so-called Age of the Messiah to dawn at any moment. The signs of the times were such that radical changes in the cosmic and political structures were thought to be imminent. Paul knew all about colonialism, acculturation, cross-cultural conflict and communication, incipient nationalism, and the burning desire for freedom, respectability, and status.

The fact is that Paul's world (Greek and Roman as well as Jewish) was in turmoil. The Graeco-Roman world especially was a seething cauldron of new religions, nationalism, social change, stress, apocalyptic hope, economic tyranny, and political manoeuvring. Men everywhere were looking for salvation, and roads to salvation were two-a-penny.[2]

To this world Paul came with the Gospel of Jesus Christ. Paul himself had been obliged to rethink and re-examine his whole rabbinic theology in the searing light of the irrefutable fact that Jesus of Nazareth lives. His total understanding of the Old Testament had to be revised and reviewed at the foot of the cross and outside the empty tomb. Once he had made that traumatic transition, Paul, as the appointed apostle to the Gentiles (Acts 9:15), turned to the task of taking the Gospel out of its Judaeo-Christian setting, and communicating it to a people who were not Jews, to women and men who thought differently from Jews, whose language was different, whose customs and cultures were different, and whose traditions and religions were different. Some of the precipitate of Paul's reflection upon the meaning of the Gospel for non-Jews, and of his evaluation of the Gentiles' cultures, hopes, and aspirations in the light of the Gospel, is found in his letters. These letters speak more directly to the Melanesian situation than do any other New Testament writings.

Two Pauline Presuppositions

Of the many presuppositions with which Paul operated, two need to be singled out for special attention. The first is the concept of solidarity. According to Paul, man exists in solidarity with Adam and with creation. He is baptized into solidarity with Christ. The Pauline phrase which best sums up this idea of solidarity is 'through the one, the many . . .' (Rom. 5:18). So, for example, Adam is seen as incorporating in himself all humanity; Christ is spoken of as the representative of all mankind; by its actions, the human race is said to have affected adversely the whole creation.[3]

For Paul, the idea of solidarity is not merely an interesting aspect of anthropology or sociology. Rather, as Oscar Cullmann has pointed out, Paul believes that the solidarity relationship is determined throughout history by the theological principles of election and representation.[4] It is as divinely-appointed representative that Adam appears in creation and fall. Likewise, it is as divinely-appointed Mediator and Saviour that Christ, by virtue of his resurrection, appears in the new creation.

The second Pauline presupposition which is especially significant for our study is the understanding or conviction which Paul has concerning the relationship which exists between the past, the present, and the future. He is especially interested in the events which took place 'in the beginning', and how they relate to present realities and to future hopes and expectations. A survey of Paul's writings shows that the apostle quite consistently makes a practice of identifying present problems of existence and of offering solutions to those problems, by using as models the conditions and events which are described in the accounts of the origins of either mankind or of the people of Israel.[5] Thus, for example, when in Rom. 1:18-32 Paul wishes to describe man as he stands under the wrath of God, he uses the language and thought-patterns of the stories of the fall of Adam and of Israel. Or, again, when Paul speaks of the obedience of Christ, the second Adam, he makes use of a hymn (Phil. 2:6-11) in which Christ is implicitly contrasted with Adam.

With these preliminary remarks on the nature and scope of the biblical material which will serve as the basis and catalyst for the task before us, we are almost ready to engage in theological reflection upon the religious phenomenon known as cargo cults. But one more thing needs to be said by way of an explanation, or an apology if you like.

The philosophy or ideology of cargo cults has never been expressed in written form by a believer or follower of the cults. Other ideologies have their spokesmen, their theoreticians, their apologists, who publish their ideas and theories, and engage Christian theologians in dialogue and debate (for example, the Christian theologian Moltmann and the Marxist philosopher Bloch together have probed the future of hope). But not cargoism. No cargo cultist has ever committed to paper a systematic statement of his presuppositions, objectives, hopes, and aspirations. Everything which has been published on cargo cults and cargoism has been written by non-believers. What does this mean for the interpreter? It means, among other things, that he runs the risk of being doubly wrong: wrong in his perception of what cargoism is, and understands itself to be; and wrong in his interpretation of what he perceives is cargoism's understanding of itself. Obviously, then, what follows in the remainder of this chapter must be regarded as exploratory, tentative, and more-than-usually open to debate and correction.

Cargo Cults as Quest for Identity

Cargo cults may be understood as an expression of man's quest for identity. Insofar as this is an important element in the cults, one could agree with Strauss' judgment that cargo cults are essentially anthropocentric.[6] But this judgment must be hedged somewhat. First, the man-centred nature of cargo cults should not mislead one to the conclusion that we are dealing here with cults of the individual. On the contrary, we must recognize that cargo cults are always socio-centric; that is, they are concerned with the whole group, not with any individual member of the group. Secondly, it should be borne in mind that the anthropocentric nature of the cargo cults consists not in their placing of earthlings in the centre of ritual and worship, but in the central position which is accorded the ancestors (who are regarded as men) in the scheme of things. Cargoism holds that the ancestors are responsible for man's loss of identity; at the same time, the ancestors are thought to be the only ones who can resolve the identity crisis in which Melanesian man finds himself.

Cargo cults are evidence for the existence of an awareness that man's present condition is not what it could or should be, and that things were not always as they are now. The reason for this situation is that in the mythical past, Melanesian man made certain decisions and performed certain actions which altered his status, made him inferior to other men, and deprived him of the means and opportunity to attain to that desirable condition known in theological language as 'salvation'.

Students of cargo cults differ in their understanding of the nature of the original actions and decisions which led to the forfeiture of man's true identity and self-respect. Kenelm

Burridge (in his analysis of the primal myth which tells of the original, seminal acts which had such drastic consequences for later generations) speaks of moral responsibility, moral imperatives, moral and immoral relationships and behaviour. According to Burridge, the Tangu believe that their progenitor committed an act of disobedience, a 'sin' which had certain consequences, and which bore certain fruit. Punishment had to be suffered; guilt had to be acknowledged and borne; forgiveness had to be sought and obtained; atonement for sin had to be made.[7]

Peter Lawrence, on the other hand, places far less emphasis on the idea of an early sin and subsequent guilt on the part of the Melanesians. He, in fact, regards the concept of sin as quite foreign to the people of the Southern Madang district. He writes:

> There is nothing to suggest that the natives were beginning to fear lest they were morally unworthy . . . Even in cargo doctrine there was no hint that the natives' present economic inferiority was due to the sinfulness of their forebears. The ancestors . . . were portrayed as obtuse rather than evil. They took the wrong turnings on the road mapped out for them, and their mistakes were far more in the nature of 'cosmic bad luck' than a permanent fall from grace in an ethical or spiritual sense.[8]

In Lawrence's view, the people of the Southern Madang district attribute the loss of their cargo inheritance, including the loss of their authentic identity, to acts of foolishness and stupidity on the part of the ancestor/s, or to a combination of circumstances over which the forebears had no control.

One way or another — either through a sinful action or a foolish one, or both — man lost his identity, his status, and his self-respect. There lives in Melanesia the hope that a time is coming when the fateful decisions and actions which were taken in the past will somehow be reversed, and man will regain his true identity, his dignity and integrity as a human being. This will happen, it is believed, when a cargo movement is actually brought to a successful conclusion. Burridge says:

> A cargo movement asks for repentance and holds out the promise of forgiveness, expiation, and atonement; it offers a share in the cargo; it assures participants of a new life, a new dispensation which will take the place of the old.[9]

One particular feature of the quest for identity which ought to be given special attention is the desire and felt need for men to achieve 'big-man' status in the community. It is essential for the well-being of the group that at least one of their number is a 'big-man'. A 'big-man' has special powers and specialized knowledge which enables him to function as a mediator between the people and the ancestors or deities, and to direct the various ritualistic activities of the group. One of the duties and functions of the 'big-man' is to initiate and maintain a proper relationship between the community and the deities. The salvation of the entire group ultimately depends on the ability of the 'big-man' to operate skilfully and successfully as a mediator of right relationships and of good order in the society. [10]

Theological Perspective: A Search for Renewal

The hopes and longings for a restoration of what is thought to be man's true self may be understood theologically as a search for the renewal of the divine image and glory in man. The Apostle Paul assumed that man originally rejoiced in the possession of the glory and image of God. The divine image and glory was an integral part of man's being, of his existence as a man. Pauline (indeed, all biblical) theology defines the authentic *homo sapiens* as one who is created in the image and glory of God. One important element in the possession of the divine image and glory is the lordship which man was to exercise over and within creation. As the image and glory of God on earth, man was supposed to function as God's vice-regent, ruling over creation and the creatures.

Pauline anthropology assumes, as we have said, that man originally possessed the image and glory of God. Paul, however, also assumes that the decisions and actions of the progenitor (Adam/Israel) resulted in the loss of the glory of God and a defacing of the divine image. The apostle draws on the history of Adam, and of Israel as a nation, to show that the man who lives in solidarity with Adam or Israel has indeed lost the glory of God, and possesses, at best, only a faint shadow of the true image of God. [11] In essence, Paul is saying that the man of the old humanity is no longer true man; he has lost his real identity. The man of the old age is only a poor likeness; he is almost a caricature of the man God intended him to be.

Linked with man's loss of identity was his failure to exercise the dominion which God had given him over creation, and the subsequent ruinous exchanges which occurred in the good order which God had ordained (Rom. 1:18-26; 8:19-21). The solidarity in sin of man and creation puts them both in a situation which is a complete distortion and perversion of God's intentions. As God's vice-regent on earth, man was to rule over the 'birds and beasts and creeping things'. Instead, Adam and Israel dethroned the Creator and enthroned the creature (Rom. 1:23,25). They set up the creatures as objects of obedience and worship.

One consequence of man's abdication was that a number of powers in the cosmos, powers which were structurally 'neutral', became hostile to man. These created powers, such as the stars and the planets, began to dominate and direct man's existence, and to alienate him even further from his Creator. The powers of 'suprasolar space' (Karl Heim) held man in thrall; he lived in terror of a closed universe. Even more mundane things like rocks and pools and mountains became objects of fear and reverence. Spirits benevolent and malevolent dominated man's existence. In short, man lost control.

Man's loss of control, his relinquishing of dominion in the world, is related to his loss of the divine image and glory. One could ask whether, perhaps, the devotees of Melanesian cargo cults are expressing in their myths and rituals some of the frustration which man feels because of the loss of the divine glory and the subsequent giving up of dominion over creation. Man tries to reassert his rule by a ritualistic manipulation of the powers which are believed to control the creative processes. The special objects of man's attention are those powers which are thought to regulate the supply of all the good things required for the good life. These good things are given the collective name 'cargo'. Cargo is a symbol. It includes such things as money, freedom from hunger and death, release from the pressures and frustrations of work, the regaining of status and dignity as a man, and the effortless acquisition of knowledge and power. 'Cargo' may be understood as the Melanesian word for salvation.

Christian theology may affirm the Melanesian search for a lost identity. But it directs a man to find his true self in the person of Jesus Christ, for he is the true image and glory of God. This particular point is emphasized at several places in the Pauline epistles. In 2 Cor. 3:18 - 4:6, where Paul appears to be presenting his Christology in terms of the Old Testament story of the creation of mankind and/or of Israel, Christ is plainly described as the image and glory of God. The fundamental issue in this portion of the Corinthian correspondence is: Where is true glory to be found? Is it to be found in the Law or in the Gospel? Or, to put the question another way: Where does God reveal his glory? The answer of Judaism was that God's glory is revealed in the Torah; the people of the Torah — the Jews — see God's glory, and have at least the potential to possess the image of God. Paul responds by showing that Judaism's view of the Torah placed the Law in a false position in the divine economy of salvation. It is in the Gospel, or more precisely in Christ, that the glory of God is revealed (2 Cor. 4:4b). It is the Christian community which can see (or, which reflects) the glory of God, because their faces are unveiled. In this way they stand in contrast to the people of the synagogue, who still sit and listen to Moses with veils over their minds. It is the Christian community which has the image of God, or, as Paul puts it, 'are being changed into his likeness from one degree of glory to another'.

Just what is Paul saying here about Christ as the image and glory of God? First, he is saying that Christ's glory both reveals to man the glory of God, and shows man the nature into which he himself is to be transformed. A similar thought is expressed in Rom. 8:29:

> For those whom he foreknew he also predestined to be conformed to the image of his Son.

Likewise, in Phil. 3:21, Paul assures his readers that God will change their lowly bodies 'to be like the body of his glory'. According to Paul, the believer is to possess that image and glory of God which the glorified and exalted Lord Jesus has now.

We note, secondly, that Paul likens the illumination which the Gospel brings, to a new creative act of God:

> For it is the God who said, 'Let light shine out of darkness', who has shone in our hearts to give the light of the knowledge of the glory of God in the face of Christ (2 Cor. 4:6).

God who by divine fiat caused the first light to appear in the primeval darkness has, by a new creative act, placed in the hearts of men the illumination brought by the glory of God in the face of Jesus. The true glory of God is found, not by looking back to the old creation, but by beholding the new creation as it has dawned in Christ Jesus.

Further expression of Paul's views on Christ as the image and glory of God is found in the hymn recorded in Col. 1:15-20. In the translation of the Jerusalem Bible it reads:

> He is the image of the unseen God
> and the first-born of all creation,
> for in him were created
> all things in heaven and on earth:
> everything visible and everything invisible,
> Thrones, Dominations, Sovereignties, Powers —
> all things were created through him and for him.
> Before anything was created, he existed,
> and he holds all things in unity.
> Now the Church is his body,
> he is its head.
> As he is the Beginning,
> he was the first to be born from the dead,
> so that he should be first in every way;
> because God wanted all perfection
> to be found in him
> and all things to be reconciled through him and for him,
> everything in heaven and everything on earth,
> when he made peace
> by his death on the cross.

The first part of this hymn speaks of the relationship between Christ and creation; the second part speaks of the relationship between Christ and salvation. Creation and salvation are related through 'the beloved Son' (Col. 1:13), who is Jesus Christ our Lord.

The hymn contains a number of expressions descriptive of 'the beloved Son'. The first title ascribed to the Son is 'the image of the unseen God' (Col. 1:15a). This expression must be understood against the background provided by Gen. 1:26,27 and its interpretation in Judaism. According to the Genesis passage, God made man in the divine image. The phrase 'image of God' is, thus, a description of a human being. True humanness consists in the possession of the image of God. God intended man to be 'image of God'. In the Old Testament and in early Judaism, angels are not said to have been created in the image of God; nor are animals or birds said to possess the divine image. To man alone belongs the title: Image of God. It would seem, then, that when Paul ascribes to Jesus Christ the title 'image of God', he is confessing that Christ is that true man which God created Adam to be; in Christ we see what God intended men to be when he set about making them in his own image. At the same time, of course, Christ as the image of God also reveals God to us. Hence, the phrase 'image of God', when applied to Christ, has a divine and human reference. In order to see God, we look to Christ. We must also look to Christ to see man as God intended him to be. Jesus is the whole, complete person whom men seek to be. In him we see man stripped of the sin which disfigures and scars him; we see man in his real identity. Long ago Blaise Pascal said it well when he wrote:

Without Jesus Christ we know neither our own life nor death, neither God nor ourselves.

Christ, image of God and glory of God, is the head of a new humanity, a new creation. To any man who belongs to this new creation, to any man who is 'solid' with him, Christ mediates the true image and glory of God. Men enter into a solidarity relationship with Christ by means of Baptism, which, according to Paul, is a new creative act, parallel to the Exodus and to God's creating activity in the beginning.[12] Above all, Baptism is connected with the resurrection of Jesus Christ, which in itself is a mighty creative act of God. By Baptism the man who is 'in Christ' shares in the victorious death and resurrection of the ascended Lord; he is liberated from the power of sin and death and the condemnation of the Law (1 Cor. 15:56,57). All this is possible because of the believer's union with Christ, the conqueror of all hostile powers.

Thus, the Christian is being transformed into the image and glory of Christ. That is to say, the man who is one with Christ is regaining his identity as a man. For the true man is one who, like his Ancestor the Second Adam, possesses the image and glory of God.

What is man? Pontius Pilate answered that question accurately when he pointed to Jesus Christ and said: 'Ecce Homo!' (John 19:5). In Christ man sees himself as he should be. What Jesus Christ is, Christians hope to become. On this point, tension arises between cargo ideology and Christian theology. If the authentic identity of a man is to be seen in Jesus Christ, and if in Christ Melanesian man will find his true self, then it is important to know what kind of man Jesus Christ is. What is his identity as a man? What was his life-style? Just what kind of people are Christians aspiring to become?

Jesus sought not to manipulate God but to obey him (Matt. 4:1-11). Jesus became a 'big-man' by humbling himself and becoming a servant (Phil. 2:5-8). In the Kingdom which Jesus ushered in, he taught that real status belongs to those who serve, not to those who are served; it belongs to those who humble themselves, not to those who seek to be exalted; it belongs to those who are least, not to those who are most. Christ was identified as the poor man, the humble one, the quiet one, the suffering servant of God, the friend of the outcasts and the riffraff of Jewish society. He was, indeed, a 'big-man', a ruler, but his rule required a radical reinterpretation of the meaning of status and identity:

> He has shown strength with his arm,
> he has scattered the proud in the imagination of their hearts,
> he has put down the mighty from their thrones,
> and exalted those of low degree;
> he has filled the hungry with good things,
> and the rich he has sent empty away
> (Luke 1:51-53).

These words from the *Magnificat* describe the inversion of values to which Christ commits the members of the Kingdom. Men and women who belong to Christ, who share his identity — that is, people who are truly human — are obliged to work for the principle of God's rule announced in the New Testament: 'He resists the proud and shows favour toward the humble' (1 Pet. 5:5, *translation mine*).

This is a hard saying for all men, not only for Melanesians. It means that while Christian theology may affirm the Melanesian search for identity, it must at the same time issue the caveat that the true identity of a man — the one found in Jesus Christ — is somewhat the opposite to the kind of identity for which

Melanesians traditionally strive. In effect, then, Christian theology challenges both the road by which Melanesians search for their identity, and the understanding which Melanesians have of the kind of identity for which they are searching.

The Role of the Ancestors

A second significant feature of the search for salvation in Melanesia is the belief that it is the ancestor or ancestors who will inaugurate the golden age, the age of salvation. Perhaps this expectation lies at the very heart of the cargo cults.

One thing Christianity and traditional Melanesian religions have in common is the conviction that the dead are not dead at all, but are alive. The Melanesian view, however, goes much further than the Christian in spelling out the relationship which exists between the living who have died and the living who have not yet died. Traditional Christianity sings:

> The saints on earth and those above
> But one communion make . . .
> One family we dwell in Him,
> One Church above, beneath;
> Though now divided by the stream,
> The narrow stream of death.

In practice, the theology of the communion which exists between the living and the saints who have died in the Lord seems to have little meaning in the lives of earth-bound Christians. That, perhaps, describes the situation in Protestantism more so than in Catholicism.

In the Melanesian world, the ancestral spirits are part and parcel of the existence of the living, and they have a place in the social system. The manner in which the living and the ancestors relate one to the other is well described by Roderic Lacey in his analysis of the Enga world view, which he summarizes as follows:

1. A person does not live in isolation as a single individual. His life, identity, and way of acting flow from the heritage which has come to him through many generations of ancestors. He and his ancestors are sharers in this common life.
2. Man lives in a community made up not only of men and women who are now alive and present with him, but in a community of men and spirits, all of whom are alive. Some of these persons, because they are spirits and hence their power is not so restricted as it was when they were men, are more powerful than others. One needs to relate to these persons in a balanced way.
3. Life is a continual, changing, and dynamic pattern of relationships between persons, some men, some spirits; all living. The good life is lived by maintaining appropriate relationships with the proper people.[13]

One point in the above statement which needs to be emphasized is that the spirits are not restricted in their power and activity as are the living. This thought was touchingly expressed by an old man when speaking of his duty to look after his sons. He said:

> I am looking forward to the day of my death. When I am dead it will be much easier for me to care for my sons. Right now I grow weary of the constant worry of watching over my children while I am in the body.

The members of the community who are no longer earth-bound, the spirits, the ancestors, are the ones who hold the key to the good life. Cargoism expresses and nourishes the hope that one day soon the ancestors, who have already gained access to the secret of the good life, will share with the living the benefits and blessings to which they have already attained. In a limited way they are already doing this. But, for various reasons, the road is not as open as it could or should be.

The ancestor (or the ancestors, viewed collectively) does not share in the present unhappy earthly existence of the Melanesians. Hence, he may be regarded as one from outside of the group. Yet he is by no means an 'outsider'. He is often thought of as the progenitor or founder of the clan. He is the one member of the community who possesses the power, the ability, and the knowledge necessary to effect the radical changes which are expected to take place in the cosmic and social structures. Hence, in Melanesian thought, salvation depends upon the intervention and cooperation of one (individual ancestor or group) who is a member, and yet not a member, of the group which awaits salvation. He is in a sense supra-historical, yet he shares in the warp and woof of everyday life. He is a part of this world, and yet apart from it.

Theological Critique: The Way of Salvation

From the point of view of Pauline theology, we must say that the Melanesian search for salvation will always end in frustration as long as the hopes are centred on the ancestors. On this point there is fundamental disagreement between Christianity and cargoism.

According to cargo ideology, the gaining of salvation depends upon the society's ability to create conditions which will induce the ancestors to play their decisive part in bringing about a restoration and renewal of all things. According to Paul, however, a renewal of the divine image and glory, the granting of life and salvation, and the beginning of the new creation depend entirely upon the action of God in Christ Jesus. Apart from him, all hopes are empty.

The crux of the matter is the 'way' of salvation. When man finds himself in an extreme situation he asks: 'What is to be done?' and: 'What shall I do to be saved?' The classical answer to those questions is that man must do something. He has recourse to magic, to ritual, to various ways of manipulating the powers who are thought to be responsible for the presence or absence of salvation. And he must make sure that his own life and the lives of all others in his society conform to appropriate patterns of behaviour. Taboos must be strictly observed; laws must be scrupulously obeyed; good order must be established and maintained. Above all, proper relationships must be preserved between man and man, and between man and the deities or spirits.

Relationships in Melanesia are controlled by the concept of what in Pidgin is called *lo*. This word *lo* covers a wider semantic field than does the English word 'law'. According to Theodor Ahrens, the word *lo* means:

> the moral actions and social behaviour accepted and expected by a group, kept secret from other groups, endorsed by the forefathers and approved by the ancestral spirits.[14]

Thus, *lo* can refer to a religious rite which establishes relationships with the spirits and the deities; it can refer to legal obligations which exist between a man and his wife's relatives; or it can refer to the stabilization of trade practices between two villages. *Lo* is anything which establishes and delineates a relationship within a group or with ancestors or deities. Obviously, then, *lo* regulates all aspects of life. *Lo* may also signify an obligation on both sides of a relationship, which makes the relationship interdependent and reciprocal. In this sense, *lo* almost has the meaning of 'contract' or 'agreement'.

Ancestors or deities are, usually, either a partner in the relationship which is established by *lo*, or they are expected to safeguard the fulfilment of *lo*. If *lo* is properly observed, then the ancestors and deities must keep their part of the agreement: they must meet their obligations. Thus, if, in connection with gardening activities, *lo* is observed by the ones who plant and till the gardens, then the spirits and deities who control fertility must reciprocate by ensuring a bountiful harvest. If, on the other hand, *lo* relationships are neglected or despised, then misfortune, failure of harvest, loss of power and security may be expected.

It is of the essence, then, that *lo* relationships and obligations are established, preserved, endorsed, and fulfilled in every sphere of life. If all this is done to perfection, then there is a good chance that salvation will be achieved.[15]

The Christian and the traditional Melanesian 'way' of salvation are poles apart. There is, moreover, a dimension to Christian salvation-hope which was unknown in old Melanesia. Christian salvation is concerned, first and foremost, with man's relationship to God the Creator, Sustainer, and Judge of all. Paul (indeed, all biblical theology) teaches that the proper relationship between man and God has been tragically twisted and put out of joint. Man is not right with God. This 'not-rightness' between man and God is reflected in the distorted and chaotic conditions which obtain in the relationships between man and man, and between man and the other creatures which God has made. Where there should be peace, harmony, order, amity, and balance, there is, instead, tension, animosity, disunity, disorder, and disturbance. In Melanesian terms, a state or condition of *lo* does not exist.

The Good News is that God has acted in and through his Son Jesus Christ to put right all that has gone wrong, to restore proper relationships between himself and man, between man and man, and between man and creation. Sin which separated man from God has been dealt with; the powers which set God and man and creation at odds have had their teeth removed; the chaos which tended to rule in the old created orders is being turned into good order once again. All this is a consequence and result of what God has done, and does, through his beloved, Jesus Christ.

The situation now is that it is neither possible nor necessary for man to attempt to walk the tightrope of life, constantly juggling the various components which threaten to thwart his search for salvation. There is no need, nor is it possible, for man to try to manipulate God, and to force him into a position where he is obliged to grant to man the salvation for which he is striving. The message which God's ambassadors announce to all men is:

> God in Christ was reconciling the world to himself, not holding men's faults against them, and he has entrusted to us the news that they are reconciled . . . and the appeal . . . is: be reconciled to God! (2 Cor. 5:19,20, JB).

These words of Paul pinpoint the two areas in which there is fundamental disagreement between Christianity and cargoism: salvation is God's gracious activity for man through the mediatorship of Jesus Christ. Salvation is not an act of man whereby he so orders matters that the powers which control salvation are obliged to act in man's favour. Essentially, then, the confrontation between Christianity and cargoism resolves itself into a replay of the old, old question: Is salvation a state or condition which man achieves, or helps to achieve, for himself?

Or, is it something which comes to man outside of himself, from a gracious God, 'without money and without price'? The answer to those questions encapsulates the difference between Christian faith and cargoism.

Yet, despite the fundamental difference, there is perhaps what the Germans call an *Anknüpfungspunkt*, a point of contact, an area of agreement between Pauline theology and Melanesian cargo ideology. In Melanesia, the hopes for salvation are expected to be realized by the action of the ancestor/s, coming into the present and acting favourably on man's behalf. This basic Melanesian belief has its theological counterpart in the so-called Adamic Christology of the Apostle Paul. For the sake of making our point, we must give this particular aspect of Pauline theology more than just a passing nod.

Christ and Adam

A glance at a concordance under the entry 'Adam' indicates that the name of the first man occurs only three times in the Pauline writings. [16] This bare statistical fact is misleading. From it one could obtain a wholly-inadequate notion of the importance of Adam for Paul's thought. The conception of Christ as the Second Adam plays a far more important part in the thought of the apostle than the scanty references to Adam would lead us to suppose.

Paul first introduces the Adam/Christ typology in connection with a discourse on the resurrection in the 15th chapter of his first Corinthians letter. He begins his exposition by establishing the historical character of the resurrection of Christ. Then, using the figure of the first fruits, Paul shows that Christ's resurrection is the first stage in the glorious resurrection of God's temple. The Adamic parallel is used to show how the resurrection of the one is the resurrection of the many:

> For as in Adam all die, so also in Christ shall all be made alive . . . As was the man of dust, so are those who are of the dust; and as is the man of heaven, so are those who are of heaven (1 Cor. 15:22,48).

Death entered through the first man who is the man of dust, whereas life reigns through the second Man who came from heaven and became a 'life-giving spirit' (v 45), conferring his life upon those who are his. It is at just this point that Jesus, the Second Adam, differs from his predecessor, Adam: Jesus is what Adam was not, that is, he is the giver of life.

The theme of 'life', together with the Adam/Christ typology, links the Corinthians chapter with the fifth chapter of Paul's Letter to the Romans. In the Romans chapter, Paul shows how God's saving verdict in Christ was a decision for God's people

(Rom. 5:5-11). The demonstration of this fact is by way of the Adamic parallel and contrast:

> Then as one man's trespass led to condemnation for all men, so one man's act of righteousness leads to acquittal and life for all men. For as by one man's disobedience many were made sinners, so by one man's obedience many will be made righteous (Rom. 5:18,19; see also 5:12).

The close relationship between the Romans and Corinthians passages is accentuated not merely by the use of the Adam/Christ typology, but especially by the point of contrast which is made in both passages. Paul contrasts Adam and Christ with regard to both their actions and the consequences of their actions. Adam's sin resulted in death for his descendants; Christ's obedience means that what lies in the future for those who belong to him is life, that life which God intended for Adam. Thus, the fifth chapter of Romans ends with the joyful affirmation that God's gift is eternal *life* through the Lord Jesus Christ. We find, then, that in their very contrasts Christ and Adam have some points of comparison. Both are agents: through Adam has come death, whereas through Christ has come life. Adam and Christ are, moreover, both founders of a race of men. Each is head of his particular humanity. Adam is the progenitor of that humanity whose end is death, while Christ is the head of the eschatological community which is appointed to life.

We must now look briefly at a little poem or hymn in which the name of Adam is not mentioned, but in which the Adam/Christ contrast is implied. Phil. 2:6-8 reads in poetic form:

> Christ Jesus . . . though he was in the form of God,
> did not count equality with God a thing to be grasped,
> but emptied himself,
> taking the form of a servant,
> being born in the likeness of men.
> And being found in human form
> he humbled himself
> and became obedient unto death,
> even death on a cross.

A survey of the available linguistic evidence indicates that the phrase 'form of God' in the first line of the hymn is to be taken as equivalent to the description which is given of the first man, Adam (Gen. 1:26,27). At his creation, Adam reflected God's glory; he was made in the divine image. At the Fall, Adam lost the glory of God and defaced the divine image. The terrible effects of Adam's sin were reversed by Jesus Christ, the Second Adam. Christ took Adam's nature upon himself (Rom.8:3), and fulfilled the role of the obedient Second Adam in whom the image of true manhood is to be seen. Thus, Christ is the new man whose image is renewed in the church (Col. 3:10).

An Adam/Christ contrast is implied in the words of the second line of the Philippians hymn: 'did not count equality with God a thing to be grasped'. The idea of a prize to be gained by snatching is precisely the bait which the serpent dangled before Eve: 'You will be like God' (Gen. 3:5b). In response to the serpent's promise, Adam, 'the son of God' (Luke 3:38), attempted to assert himself as God. Adam had been given a relative lordship (Gen. 1:28), but he wanted a complete lordship in his own right. He failed; he 'died', and he was expelled from Eden.

In contrast to Adam, Jesus Christ, the Second Adam, refused to exploit his unique place in the Godhead as the glory and image of God and to assert himself in opposition to his Father. As 'Adam in reverse', Christ refused to snatch at what lay before him, that is, a universally-acknowledged equality with God. Instead, he was obedient to the Father on the road which led to lordship by way of humiliation, suffering, and death, 'even death on a cross'.

The contrast between Christ and Adam in Phil. 2:6-8 has been set out in parallel columns for easy reference: [17]

Adam	Christ
made in the image of God	being in the form of God
thought it a prize to be grasped at	thought it not a prize to be grasped at
to be as God,	to be like God,
and strove to be of reputation	but made himself of no reputation
and spurned being God's servant,	and took upon him the form of a servant
wishing to be in the likeness of God;	and was made in the likeness of men;
and being found in human form	and being found in human form
he exalted himself	he humbled himself
and was disobedient unto death.	and became obedient unto death.

There has been some discussion concerning the origins of Paul's Adamic Christology. Some say he borrowed it from Gnosticism (but that suggestion has been proved wrong); some think he developed it from certain ideas current in rabbinic Judaism; others, again, suggest that Paul himself was the Spirit-inspired genius who thought up the concept. Whatever the answer to the question concerning the origins of the Adamic Christology, there can be little doubt about what Paul meant by it. For Paul, Jesus Christ is the man whom God intended Adam to be. Christ did all that Adam had failed to do. Christ was obedient where Adam had been disobedient. Christ exercised lordship (Phil 2:9-11) where Adam had abdicated his vice-regal position. Christ's actions mean life for men, whereas Adam's rebellion had led to death. Christ exhibits fully and completely the image and glory of God. In this, too, Adam was a failure. As ancestor, Adam brought only sorrow, pain, death, and destruction to his descendants. Christ, as ancestor, brings life, healing, wholeness, and salvation to those who belong to him.

We find, then, that Paul's Adamic Christology is a forceful reminder that Christians, too, look to the Ancestor for salvation. The Ancestor who brings salvation is not Adam, nor Israel, nor some folk-hero from the mythical or historical past. The Christian's Ancestor is the historical person, the true man, Jesus Christ. He is both the son of Adam and the son of God (Luke 3:22,28). He came and ushered in God's gracious rule on earth. He came and inaugurated the day of salvation (Luke 4:21; 19:9). He is the head of the new humanity. He is the Second Adam. He is the only Ancestor who brings salvation.

The Search for Salvation Today

At this point, a few words must be said about the nature of the salvation-hope which is expressed in the cargo cults. In particular, we focus attention on one striking feature of this hope. Salvation, in cargoist terms, is not oriented to the after-life, to the life after death, but to the here and now. Salvation, it is thought, will eventuate here, on this earth, in this present age, and it will involve all known structures of society. It is a concrete, this-worldly salvation for which Melanesians hope. Salvation means freedom from want and sickness, relief from the pressures of work and time, a state of wholeness and health, a regaining of one's prestige and self-respect, an ordering of relationships so that proper balances obtain in the social structures.

What, from the point of view of biblical theology, may be said about this pragmatic, concrete, this-worldly salvation-hope? Christian theology may affirm the search for present salvation. The Good News is that Jesus Christ is Lord in both creation and redemption now. His lordship is a present reality. He has already won salvation for men and for the universe. In a sense, 'salvation today' (to use a popular phrase of several years ago) is the only kind of salvation. There is, in fact, a sort of tautology in the phrase: 'salvation today'. You don't put salvation in your pocket and keep it for a suitable occasion. It is true that in this end-time we Christians experience the tension of the already/not yet of salvation. Consummation has not yet followed fulfilment. The New Testament speaks of salvation in both the present and the future tenses, [18] and both usages are, of course, proper and accurate. Nevertheless, in view of the tendency of preachers and teachers in Melanesia to stress the 'not yet' of salvation at the expense of the 'already' (so that we get a kind of pie-in-the-sky hope), an emphasis on the fact that the new life and the new creation were inaugurated with the resurrection of Jesus Christ is not out of place. Since all things have been reconciled (Col. 1:20), the Melanesian hope for a salvation here and now is, at least in part, a theologically-realistic expectation.

And yet, we must add that, from the perspective of Pauline theology, we cannot make unqualified affirmations about the Melanesian salvation-hope. To do so would be dishonest and an exercise in futility. There is one element in the Pauline view of salvation which is unpalatable, unpopular, and unpleasant to many: Paul insists that participation in salvation in the end-time involves a sharing in Christ's suffering. So, for example, he writes to the Philippians (3:10, JB):

> All I want is to know Christ and the power of his resurrection and to share his sufferings by reproducing the pattern of his death. That is the way I can hope to take my place in the resurrection of the dead.

And to the Romans Paul writes in similar vein (8:17, JB):

> And if we are children we are heirs as well: heirs of God and coheirs with Christ, sharing his sufferings so as to share his glory.

There can be no doubt that this is one of the more offensive aspects of the Christian message: the thought that a man cannot share Christ's glory unless he also shares his suffering and shame and cross. Some preachers deliberately omit to speak of this particular facet of the Christian life. And many people in Melanesia (as in other parts of the world) have made the twin mistakes of assuming that the road into the kingdom of God is an easy road, and that this easy road is also the 'road to cargo'. The truth is, however, as Carl Braaten writes:

> [There is no] painless access to the Kingdom of God; all things must go the way of the cross; all things must be incorporated into the death of Christ before sharing his everlasting future. [19]

Salvation for the Whole Society

A fourth feature of the Melanesian search for salvation is that the expressed hopes and expectations concern the individual not as an individual but only as a member of the group. The hopes embrace the animal world, and, in fact, all of creation. Salvation is not something which an individual can experience apart and removed from the community and the cosmos in which he lives. The achievement of the individual's salvation is always dependent upon the actions of his fellow-clansmen, his family, his ancestors, and the deities with whom he has entered into relationships of mutual dependence.[20]

One of the hopes of a cargo cultist is that he will be united in every possible way — in a saving way — with the folk-hero and the ancestors. These always have been united with the present generation in many ways, but on a supranatural level. The hope is for a reunion and sharing in salvation on this earth at this time. All members of the group will be, and must be, involved, both those living as spirits and those who are alive in the body.

Cargo movements in Melanesia are always group-movements. Under the leadership and direction of the 'big-man' who has the secret knowledge necessary to make salvation a reality, the group acts, and must act, together. The leader has imposed *lo* upon the group, and this *lo* must be strictly adhered to. An aberration on the part of one member endangers the success of the whole movement for the entire group. Gernot Fugman, in a useful analysis of Melanesian concepts of salvation, points out that even the ancestors and deities, in the interests of their own welfare, are concerned that everything is done according to *lo*. The ancestors, no less than the women and men and children and pigs living in the earthly community, are members of the group. Their own existence, their own power, their own continuity is threatened if a state of *lo* is not maintained.[21]

A communal salvation is envisaged. It is achieved by all members of the group acting in concert, and affirming their solidarity with the ancestors. In the cargo cults, this solidarity is expressed in the performance of the rites thought to be necessary to communicate with the spirits and to establish a favourable climate for the ancestors' saving activity. Some of these rites seem to be imitations of the Christian sacraments of Baptism and the Eucharist. Thus, for example, the prophet Mambu insisted that the members of his cult have their genitals sprinkled with water. A form of baptism is also practised in the Yali (or *lo bos*) movement. A common theme in the cargo cults is the communal banquets which will be held when earthlings are united with the ancestors. It is quite likely that these rituals were influenced by Christianity, but they appear to have their roots in the traditional religions.

Finally, we should note that the salvation which is envisaged is one which will affect not only the human community. There will be 'a new heaven and a new earth'. Mountains will be levelled to fertile plains. Trees will bear prodigiously all the year round. Dogs and pigs will rise from the dead. Rivers will change their courses. The earth may even be turned upside down. The result, however, will not be chaos, but order, fertility, peace, and harmony. This will be a new creation in which the new society will live in peace and prosperity for ever.

Collective Redemption: A Theological View

Christian theology may affirm the Melanesian desire for maintaining proper relationships with the ancestors, just as it may affirm the realization that redemption involves the whole group and faithful membership therein. But these things, too, must be given new content and direction. Union with the ancestor is, indeed, essential for salvation. But as we have already said, the only ancestor who brings salvation is Jesus Christ; and he, therefore, is the one Ancestor with whom we must be united if we are to have salvation. The solidarity relationship which must, and does, exist between Christ and the Christian is best expressed in the peculiarly-Pauline phrase 'in Christ', and described in the Pauline images of Christ as the first fruits, the first-born, and the Head of the Church.

'In Christ'

Even the casual reader of Paul's epistles cannot but notice the constantly-recurring phrases: 'into Christ', 'in Christ', and 'with Christ'. Scholars wage a continuing debate about the many nuances of these phrases, and about the way in which they are related one to the other. But we may say, without generating too much argument, that by the 'in-, with-, and into-Christ' expressions Paul intended to convey the idea that a close relationship exists between Christ and the individual Christian, and between Christ and the Christian community. Paul, moreover, emphasizes that the Christian's relationship with Christ does not depend on his subjective feelings or emotions, but on certain objective events in Christ's life in which the Christian somehow participates: suffering, death, burial, resurrection, and exaltation. One passage from Paul's writings may serve to illustrate this point:

> Do you not know that all of us who have been baptized into Christ Jesus were baptized into his death? We were buried therefore with him by baptism into death, so that as Christ was raised from the dead by the glory of the Father, we too might walk in newness of life. For if we have been united with him in a death like his, we shall certainly be united with him in a resurrection like his. We know that our old self was crucified with him so that the sinful body might be destroyed . . . But if we have died with Christ, we believe that we shall also live with him . . . So you also must consider yourselves dead to sin and alive to God in Christ Jesus (Rom. 6:3-11).

The meaning of these 'in-, with-, and into-Christ' phrases is probably best grasped if we understand them in the light of the concept of solidarity: a solidarity relationship exists between Christ and his community. This unique relationship is beautifully described by Paul under the figure of Christ as the first fruits and the first-born.

Christ as First Fruits and First-born

In the great resurrection chapter of First Corinthians, Paul twice calls Jesus the 'first fruits':

> Christ has been raised from the dead, the first fruits of those who have fallen asleep . . . But each in his own order: Christ the first fruits, then at his coming those who belong to Christ (1 Cor. 15:20,23).

Paul believes that there is a unity between the resurrected Christ and those Christians who have died, the same kind of unity which prevails between the first fruits and the rest of the crop. A continuity exists between the nature of the body of the resurrected Christ and the nature of the future body of the believers.

Christ is described as 'first fruits' only in the context of resurrection. Resurrection is an act of creation (Rom. 4:17); hence, in speaking of resurrection, Paul uses the vocabulary of creation-talk. This may be illustrated from Rom. 8:23:

> And not only the creation, but we ourselves, who have the first fruits of the Spirit, groan inwardly as we wait for adoption as sons, the redemption of our bodies.

A comparison between this verse and an earlier verse (8:11) indicates that it is the Spirit of God who is said to be the agent of resurrection (see Rom. 1:4) and of the creation of man's new nature ('the redemption of our bodies'). The same Spirit was active at the first creation. In the prophetic literature of the Old Testament, the Spirit was said to be the agent of the resurrection, and of that new creation which would be accomplished in the times of the Messiah.[22]

According to Paul, then, to have the first fruits of the Spirit is to have the sure hope that these poor bodies of ours (Phil. 3:21a) will one day be resurrected, recreated, changed to be like Christ's body of glory (Phil. 3:21b). The guarantor of this event, and the one who will accomplish it by his power (Phil. 3:21c) is the 'first fruits from the dead', Jesus Christ our Lord.

The thought of Christ as first fruits is paralleled and complemented by another title which Paul ascribes to Christ, namely, 'first-born'. This title is used twice in the Colossians hymn, where it is linked with creation (Col. 1:15) and with salvation (Col. 1:18). The term 'first-born' signifies primarily priority of rank. But there is also a strong element of the idea of rule, authority, power. As the 'first-born from the dead' (Col. 1:18), the Ancestor Jesus initiates and makes possible similar resurrections among his descendants.

The terms 'first-born' and 'first fruits' both imply a priority of rank, which points to the lordship of Christ. It is the risen man, the *Lord* Jesus Christ who exercises and exhibits his lordship by making possible the Christian's new existence. The terms 'first-born' and 'first fruits' also imply an identity of nature between the one who is at the head and the ones who follow. The head, Christ, is the reality of God's intention for humanity. The descendants of the Second Adam are to be conformed to the same humanity which their Ancestor Jesus Christ already possesses (Rom. 8:29). The titles 'first-born' and 'first fruits' are also one way of expressing the solidarity relationship which exists between Christ and the members of his community. They emphasize the truth that Christ is the inclusive personality of the new creation. In some way Christ mediates his own life to the believer. Thus, an indissoluble bond links the Ancestor Christ with those who by faith belong to his family of descendants.

The means by which one enters into a proper and saving relationship with the Ancestor Christ is the Sacrament of Baptism. Baptism is the place where a man shares in Christ's death and resurrection (Rom. 6:3-5). By Baptism the believer is joined in a solidarity relationship with Jesus Christ who is the Head of the new humanity.

Baptism also unites a person with a host of other women and men ('the saints on earth and those above') who by Baptism have been joined to the Body of the Ancestor and thereby share a common Lord, a common faith, and a common hope of salvation (Eph. 4:1-6). According to Paul, if a person is not a member of the Body of Christ, the Church — that which the Nicene Creed calls the 'one holy, catholic, and apostolic church' — he can have no real salvation-hope, for only those who are members of the Body share the Head's suffering and death and resurrection and glory. Understood in this way, Paul would agree with the ancient dictum: *Extra ecclesiam nulla salus* (There is no salvation outside the church).

Union with the group is an essential element in the salvation-hope. This particular emphasis in cargo ideology strikes a responsive chord in Christian theology. But Christianty must hold to the assertion that the community with whom one must be united is the Church of Jesus Christ, which is his Body (Col. 1:18,24). Within this group, Baptism, the new creative act of God's life-giving Spirit, is preserved and performed. Within this group, men have table fellowship with their Lord. In the church, the congregation, the Ancestor Jesus Christ is present among his people to bless and to save. The Church is the means Christ chose to provide a way of creating and sustaining a sense of continuity among his brothers and sisters and descendants. In and by means of the Church, our Ancestor Christ continues to break into our world, keeping the future open, and so saving men from being caught in the cramped cage of their own existence. The purpose of the presence of the Church on earth, its very *raison d'être*, is to offer hope and life with God and salvation to people who are

separated from Christ, alienated from the commonwealth of Israel, and strangers to the covenants of promise, having no hope and without God in the world (Eph. 2:12).[23]

The people of Jesus Christ are an eschatological community which awaits the coming of its Head and progenitor, the Second Adam (Phil. 3:20,21). The Church does this waiting in company with the rest of creation which, as Paul tells us, is like a little child standing on tip-toe, looking for the coming of the great day of redemption and salvation (Rom. 8:18-23). Long before modern man began to recognize the existence of an interdependent symbiotic relationship between man and creation, the biblical writers were asserting that there is a solidarity between man and the cosmos in sin and in salvation. Biblical theology long ago recognized that the human situation is the key to the cosmos. Because of man's sin, the universe was placed in subjection. Because of man's sin, the earth has been raped for the good things in it; the waters and streams and seas have been fouled, the air has been polluted, and the environment spoilt. Because of man's sin, creation suffers at the hands of man. Release from suffering will come for creation only when man's redemption is consummated. This means, in effect, that the universe, as well as man, looks to the last Adam for salvation (Rom. 8:21; see also 1 Cor. 15:42,43).

This truth is beautifully expressed in the Colossians hymn to Christ (Col. 1:15-20). The high point of this hymn is the last verse:

And through him to reconcile to himself all things,
    whether on earth or in heaven,
making peace by the blood of his cross.

With these words Paul asserts that Jesus Christ, head of the universe and Head of the Church, came to reconcile all things to God. In the first chapter of Romans, Paul describes the distortions which took place in the created order as a result of the sinful exchanges which man made. The verb which is translated 'reconcile' in Col. 1:20 implies a restitution to a previous order of things. The use of this verb here reminds us that the world was created as something good; it was ruined after the Fall, but God intends to return the universe to its pristine good order. This is the world's destiny.

In Jesus Christ the tragedy of Romans 1 is reversed. In Christ, men may find all they have lost, and all that they are properly seeking, as they are changed from the image of the earthly to the image of the heavenly (1 Cor. 15:49). The very cosmos finds its destiny linked with that of man. Both man and the universe look to Jesus Christ to make them, in the new creation, what God intended them to be in the old.

A foretaste of how all things will be, when God's saving purposes for the world are finally accomplished, is provided in miniature, so to speak, by the Church. This particular point is the highlight of the closing section of a study of Ephesians by Martin Scharlemann, entitled *The Secret of God's Plan*.[24] The Church, Scharlemann writes, is to be the precursor, the microcosm of the vast cosmic order which will be the final product of God's redemptive purposes. The unity, order and 'rightness' of things which exists in the Church as a paradigm of future total good order, is illustrated by way of the marriage relationship (Eph. 5:21-33). True unity in marriage is achieved according to a pattern which was not dreamed up by men, but which was introduced to mankind from outside his existence. God himself provided the dynamic for a new way of life in marriage, and in all other relationships, when he sent his Son into human history. In the voluntary subordination of his Son, God revealed in human history the kind of humility and subordination that heals human divisions and dissensions and brings about harmony and unity (Eph. 2:11-18). The Church is supposed to be a living reminder and living evidence of this fact. God intends his Church to serve as a unifying instrument among all the fragmentizing forces of society. Thus, the Church

> constitutes the only real exhibit of the kind of reconciliation that God has in mind for 'all things'.[25]

In Melanesia the church has tried to be that which God intended his Church to be: the place where he is present among men; the place where people may breathe the life-giving spirit of forgiveness and freedom and hope; the place where they experience the joy of being united with the Ancestor Jesus Christ, and through him with one another; the place where humility and service and suffering and concern for others are as natural as breathing. The church has tried to be such a place, but it has not always succeeded. Men have sometimes discovered that the church is something else, another kind of place. In frustration, men have turned to cargo cults and cargoism with renewed energy and zeal. They think that in cargoism they will find the answers to the problems of their existence.

We have reflected upon the essence of cargoism as a search for salvation. But, in so doing, we have made the discovery that theological reflection upon cargoism directs us to consider the nature, character, and function of the church as 'bearer of salvation'. The church in Melanesia will never understand the true theological significance and challenge of the cargo cults until it arrives at a proper theological understanding of its own existence and purpose in the world.

Chapter 5

THE RESPONSE OF THE CHURCH TO CARGO CULTS*

Cargo cults are a fact of life in Melanesia. Like urban crime and alcoholism and broken marriage and prostitution and materialism, they are one of the chronic challenges which the church must face squarely.[1] Cargo cults will not disappear if the church and her theologians pretend that the cults do not constitute a threat to Christianity, or that they simply do not exist. Churchmen need to be as realistic in their assessment of cargo cults as is the anthropologist Peter Lawrence when he writes:

> We must acknowledge and respect cargo ideology as a carefully integrated intellectual system which, as has been shown by its persistence over eighty years, is extremely durable.[2]

The ability of the cargo ideology to retain its grip on the minds and hearts, even of those who have been Christians for many years, is an indication of how much the aims of cargo cults answer to deep-rooted imperatives in Melanesian life and culture.

This chapter (which takes the form of a programmatic essay) outlines specific steps which I believe the churches in Melanesia could take in their attempt to respond in a positive and constructive way to the challenge of cargo cults. These steps may be summarized under three heads: First, an effort must be made to understand the cults, the cultists, and their ideology. Secondly, the churches must initiate a rigorous program of self-examination, especially with regard to their attitudes to, and treatment of, cargo cultists. Thirdly, specific action must be taken to improve the effectiveness of ministry to cargo cultists and to those within the cargo ambit.

---

* A German version of this chapter has been prepared for *Theologische Beiträge aus Papua Neuguinea,* Horst Bürkle ed. (Erlangen: Verlag der Evang.-Luth. Mission in Erlangen).

I

Before we proceed to consider possibilities for the future, it may be helpful to gain perspective by examining briefly the question of how in the past the church has responded to cargo cults. For this purpose I have chosen two examples of 'official' responses to cargo cults by the two major church bodies in Melanesia: the Catholic and the Lutheran churches.

The first example is taken from a little booklet entitled *Manuale Missionariorum*, written by, or in the name of, Bishop Leo Scharmach of Rabaul. The manual, which was published in 1953, has as its stated purpose (p 1):

> to give new Missionaries a knowledge of native psychology and to lay down the guiding principles to be followed in the work of reform and conversion.

The book is divided into four parts. The first three sections offer an analysis of native psychology, and rules or directions for missionary work among the people of Melanesia. The fourth part is headed, suggestively, 'Cargo Madness'. In this section, Bishop Scharmach first gives a general description of cargo cults, citing examples from New Britain and Manus. He then proceeds to analyse what he calls the 'logic of this cargo madness', and the consequences which outbreaks of cargo cults have in a society. Finally, the Bishop advises how the missionary should respond to a particular cargo movement. He says that 'cargo madness' in its acute stage must be dealt with by the government. The ring-leaders must be arrested, and law-breakers must be punished. After this, the missionary will be in the position to 'replace the false logic of cargo madness by a positive teaching'. This positive teaching is (p 65):

1. Intensive and extensive instruction about the souls of the deceased, personal judgement, hell and heaven. Positive help for souls: Prayer, Mass, Holy Communion. Limited power of souls: God the One true Creator of all things.
2. True revelation is God's Word.
   Christ is God, He became man and rose from the dead. He has told us the truth and set up His Church to communicate His teaching to us.
3. Ultimate futility of material cargo.
   Christ has given us the most precious of all food — His own body and blood.
   He has also promised us a heavenly 'cargo' in comparison with which earthly 'cargo' is nothing. Indeed, 'woe to the rich on earth'. Moreover this heavenly cargo is a supernatural gift. Mysteries impress the native more than dry scientific statements. Earthly prosperity is the fruit of hard work by competent men.
4. All authority comes from God, the Supreme Lord and Master. Therefore the Government has its authority from God. Christ is our King; He calls everyone of us to follow Him as a true and faithful soldier in His army.
   God's justice and His judgements.

Bishop Scharmach concludes that such positive teaching must replace the 'cargo madness'. But, he says:

to make the Missionary's work possible, and to prevent it being spoiled again, prompt, vigorous, and just intervention is essential.

Those are the concluding words of the book.

It is probably unfair and counter-productive to subject this Catholic document, written almost a quarter-century ago, to detailed criticism. Perhaps I may draw attention to some of the more obvious points. The first thing we notice is that the missionary is advised to make use of the law (the government) to break up a cargo movement, and to reduce it, as the Bishop explicitly says, 'to a condition the Missionary can deal with'. Cargo cults are something for the church to 'deal with'. There is no suggestion that they are to be listened to, communicated with, or understood on their own terms; they are to be dealt with. The church has the Truth which must replace the cargo ideology in its entirety.

We may note, furthermore, that the Melanesian desire for material possessions is treated as something inferior, and the Melanesian means for getting 'cargo' is dismissed with a piece of Western rationalization. Bishop Scharmach seems to be suggesting that the appropriate theological response to cargo cults is to direct the thinking of the people away from material possessions to spiritual goods and blessings. And the practical reply to cargo cults is to insist on the rational argument that 'earthly prosperity is the fruit of hard work by competent men'. Quite apart from the validity or invalidity of the theological presuppositions involved here, neither response evidences an appreciation of the Melanesian way of thinking. Melanesians do not readily accept a dichotomy between the material and the spiritual. Material and spiritual goods both come from the same source, and both are of value for this life. Likewise, the contention that earthly blessings are the result of hard work by competent men is quite unacceptable to the Melanesian in the light of his own observation that of the Europeans who had an abundance of earthly blessings, some were quite incompetent, and many appeared to do no work at all — at least, nothing that the Melanesian would call work!

Lastly, we may note that the theological approach to the treatment of cargo cults avoids facing up to the real and basic tension between Christianity and cargo cults. The question which every cargo cultist has to answer is: Who is my lord? Is Jesus Christ my creating and redeeming Lord? Or do I look to other ancestors for salvation?

From the 1953 Catholic response to cargo cults, we move to a consideration of a Lutheran response which was produced more than a decade later. In October 1964 the general synod of the Evangelical Lutheran Church of New Guinea adopted a statement concerning cargo cults. This statement was apparently intended to serve as a kind of personal confession by individual members of the church over against cargo cults. A *Kâte*, as well as an English version, produced by an expatriate missionary (the Revd W. Flierl), had been in circulation some years prior to 1964. However, the minutes of the general synod were written in Pidgin; it is the Pidgin version, therefore, which must be regarded as the official version (see Appendix). I give here an English translation of the official Pidgin version:

A Statement of Faith to Correct False Ideas about Cargo

I am a member of the church of Jesus Christ and I believe his holy Word. I therefore confess that:

1. God created all the things which are in this world, and they are here to serve my physical needs.
2. God says that I must apply myself diligently to the work he has given me to do and earn my daily bread with sweat and toil.
3. Therefore I place my trust in God, I work and I pray, and I thank God for his blessing.

****

4. There is no way in which a man can obtain manufactured articles, money, or other material goods from cemeteries, mountains, lakes or holes in the ground.
5. Therefore, I must not pray [to the dead] in cemeteries. I must not speculate about different ways of obtaining cargo. I must not try to induce fits of shaking and quivering. I must not prepare a place in the bush to pray [for cargo]. I must not pursue cargo through dreams and in many other ways. These things are nothing but illusions and deceptions of Satan.
6. If I see people doing these things or if I hear people talking in this way, I will not believe them. I will reject what they say and do. They are ignorant and misguided people.
7. Sometimes a person says: I have heard the voice of an angel; or he says that a message came to him on the wind and he heard it when he was praying; or he says that in a dream he received a prophetic message or that he communicated with a spirit. This is a trick of Satan himself.
8. Therefore, I will not listen to anyone who tries to promote cargo activity. Instead, I will expose him before the congregation and oppose all such foolish ideas. I am a member of the church of God, and now I want to stand fast on the Word of God and fight against the lies of Satan.

May Christ the Lord help me and give me his strength to defeat foolish ideas about how to get cargo.

As we review the salient points of this confessional statement, we notice that, although the declaration is said to be made on the basis of God's Word, only the first three points are theological ones — and even they do not reflect the whole of biblical teaching. Like the Catholic document we have already looked at, this Lutheran statement approached the problem of cargo cults from the standpoint of the doctrine of God the Creator, Preserver, and Judge. There is no attempt to come to grips with cargo ideology on the basis of Christology.

The fourth point in the Lutheran statement is not a theological declaration but a rational argument, made from a Western viewpoint, concerning the origin of material goods. In similar vein, the seventh paragraph — concerning dreams and messages from spirits — is one which Westerners might be willing to acept, but which many Melanesians would have difficulty in assenting to *in toto*, especially in view of the numerous scriptural examples of angels bringing messages to people by means of dreams, and also in view of their own Christian experience in this matter.

The most serious weakness in the Lutheran declaration concerning cargo cults lies in its failure to be truly Lutheran, that is, to deal with the matter in terms of Law and Gospel. Notice, for example, the eighth point:

> Therefore, I will not listen to anyone who tries to promote cargo activity. Instead, I will expose him before the congregation and oppose all such foolish ideas. I am a member of the church of God, and now I want to stand fast on the Word of God and fight against the lies of Satan.

This is the only section of the statement which speaks about the Christian's relationship with the cargo cultist. Its entire thrust is Law-oriented. The cargo cultist is to be exposed before the congregation. There is no suggestion that the Christian may be able to help his brother who is caught in the web of cargoism by speaking to him not only appropriate words of judgment but also appropriate words of grace. There is no declaration by the Christian that he stands ready to listen, advise, and patiently counsel with the cultist, carefully exploring his reasons for deserting Christ and Christianity and following the cult. There is no attempt to communicate with cargo cultists on their own terms. There is no talk of building a golden bridge of repentance and forgiveness for those who see the error of their ways. In short, in its eagerness to stamp out cargo cults and cargo thinking, the Lutheran church did not listen to its pastoral heart, but adopted a statement which *in nuce* was at odds with the very genius of Lutheranism.

In the past decade or so, the churches in Melanesia have learnt a lot about themselves and about cargo cults, with the result that attitudes have changed, and the treatment of cargo cults and cargo cultists is in many quarters quite different from that recommended by, say, Bishop Scharmach in his 1953 treatise. My purpose in reviewing the two examples from the past is not to give the present generation an opportunity to engage in self-righteous hand-wringing sessions over the follies of former days. My aim is to help the present generation of Christians to understand why some of the things which are done today are done, and why changes are needed in the church.

The two examples cited remind us, furthermore, that the question of the church's response to cargo cults is no new question. The church has responded, and is responding, to cargo cults. Often the response has been one of either complete indifference or outright condemnation, and rejection of both the cult and the cultist. The church has responded! The question now before us is whether the church is able to learn from its past and to adopt a program for the future which, on the one hand, will take into account the deep-rooted appeal of cargoism and the serious threat which it chronically poses to Christianity, and, on the other hand, will let the church be true to its evangelical and pastoral calling in the world.

II

What steps should the church take to respond to cargo cults in a positive and constructive way? In the first place, the church should continue to make a serious effort to understand cargo cults. In the past, there has been a great deal of loose, and sometimes irresponsible, talk about what cargo cults are and are not. Within the church itself, the analyses of cargo cults have sometimes been superficial and even wrong, or they have been based on and controlled by the findings of anthropologists or sociologists who, although they might not be opposed to Christianity and the activities of the church, are quite rightly not concerned with arriving at an understanding of cargo cults from a theological or pastoral point of view.

It is strange that the church and its theologians have been so slow to recognize cargo cults for what they are: religious movements which deserve to be taken seriously by those interested in theology and the phenomenology of religions. During the past century, more than 600 separate items of a scholarly nature have been published on cargo cults. Included in this number are many books which study, dissect, and interpret cargo cults in anthropological, sociological, political, and psychological terms. I am not familiar with all the literature in all languages on cargo cults, but, to my knowledge, only two books have been published in English, French, or German which specifically attempt to analyse and interpret cargo cults from a theological perspective. The one, entitled *Melanesische Cargo-Kulte* (1971), was written by Friedrich Steinbauer, a Lutheran missionary for a few years in Papua New Guinea. The book is a condensation of a much larger doctoral thesis done under the direction of Professor Niels Peter Moritzen at Erlangen. In his work Steinbauer sketches an outline for a theological approach to cargo cults; the author himself would undoubtedly be the first to admit that his book is not a fully-fledged theological critique and interpretation of cargo cults.

The other book which tackles cargo cults from a specifically-theological viewpoint is a slim volume of 55 pages written by a Seventh Day Adventist missionary, Gottfried Oosterwal, and published in 1973 by the Institute of Mennonite Studies of the Associated Mennonite Biblical Seminaries. The title of Dr Oosterwal's book is *Modern Messianic Movements*; its sub-title ('Modern Messianic Movements as a Theological and Missionary Challenge') accurately describes the chief thrust of the book. Oosterwal confines himself to outlining the shape and extent of the theological and missionary challenge which the cargo cults offer the church. Steinbauer and Oosterwal have done pioneering work. But their books could only be described as an introduction to a theological interpretation and evaluation of cargo cults.

What the churches need to undertake with a sense of urgency is an in-depth, and ongoing, study of cargo cults, a study which moves in two directions. The one thrust of the study should be the recording, collating, and analysing of the religious understanding which Melanesian participants themselves have of cargoism and cargo cults. The other direction of the study should be to evaluate and express the dynamics, the motives, the beliefs, and the goals of cargo cults in theological terms. I have the impression that unless and until the ideology of cargo cults is stated in language which the church itself uses — that is, in religious or theological language — the churches will not become sensitive to cargo cults as religious movements and as a challenge and a threat to Christianity. For this reason, if for no other, cargo cults need to be examined and interpreted from a theological viewpoint, and this evaluation and interpretation needs to be communicated to, and in, the church in theological terms.

Perhaps a simple example will serve to make my point. In an earlier chapter of this book I suggested that cargo cults may be viewed theologically as a search for salvation.[3] Now the word, idea, or concept 'salvation' is not one which is part of the language of the anthropologist, the sociologist, the psychiatrist, or the political analyst. But it is a key word in the area of comparative religions and Christian theology. Hence, the statement that 'cargo cults are a search for salvation' is a theological assertion which must be evaluated and responded to in theological terms. One could reasonably expect that when theologians and churchmen hear the statement, 'Cargo cults are a search for salvation', they will recognize that the speaker is speaking their language, and that he is claiming that cargo cults are rightly or wrongly intruding on the church's domain.

It should be noted and thankfully acknowledged that a beginning to the kind of study and research which is proposed in the previous paragraphs has been made by the staff of the Melanesian Institute for Pastoral and Socio-Economic Service at Goroka in the Eastern Highlands Province of Papua New Guinea. Some of the results of their labours have been published in their journals (Catalyst and Point), and shared with participants in orientation courses. But their work in connection with cargo cults has been piecemeal, somewhat uncoordinated, and obviously handicapped in one respect: the staff comprises anthropologists, sociologists, and theologians from the mainline churches in Melanesia, but they are all non-Melanesians. This lessens the effectiveness of the Melanesian Institute as a group fully equipped to conduct the kind of study envisaged in this essay. Participation, leadership, and direction by Melanesians is a desideratum for a fruitful religious and theological study of cargo cults.

The first task of the church, then, as it seeks to respond to cargo cults, is to try to understand the cults for what they are, and to express this understanding in language which will bring home to the churches the religious nature of the cults. One may expect that the attempt to understand the cargo cults will generate a willingness to communicate with them. It has been proved over and over again that outright condemnation and rejection of the hopes and longings which are expressed in the cargo ideology are not the first step toward establishing effective communication links with the cultists. Surely there ought to be a striving to affirm at least some aspects of the cargoists' hopes and aspirations, a recognition that many of them are legitimate even though they need refocusing and redirecting. Where at all possible, we need to make affirmations, not pronounce anathemas.

The second part of the church's response to cargo cults is perhaps even more important than the first. The church needs to look at itself and its own preaching, teaching, and practice. The charge cannot be sustained that the Christian proclamation is the root cause of cargoism and cargo cults. Nevertheless, it is a fact of history that a misunderstanding of the Christian message has precipitated, and added fuel to the fires of, cargo enthusiasm. Likewise, it cannot be proved one way or another that the church's practice in dealing with cargo cults has helped to control them, or to eradicate them, or simply to drive them underground. But it would have to be admitted that the church generally has not been conspicuously successful in its dealings with cargo cults and cultists.

To demonstrate the need for self-examination in preaching and teaching, and to take a concrete example as a kind of case-study, let us consider the question of what happened when Christian eschatology met Melanesian eschatology as it is expressed in cargo ideology. Gottfried Oosterwal has put forward the proposition that the 'creative centre' of a cargo movement is its eschatology.[4] The proposition is open to debate, but one can hardly deny that there is a Melanesian brand of eschatology, and that it is an important facet of cargoism. Included in cargo eschatology is the expectation that the society will in some way return to its source and that the golden age of the mythical or historical past will be restored. This restoration of the golden age will be preceded by cataclysms and catastrophes which will usher in and herald the return of the ancestor-hero. He will rule the resurrected dead and the living who have been changed. His rule will be characterized by truth, justice, righteousness, and equality. In this new time, there will be no sickness, no poverty, no death, no want. The dawning of the new age will affect not only the community; there will be a new heaven and a new earth. Great changes will take place in the shape and structure of the cosmos and of society. The earth may even be turned upside down. Certainly, there will be many instances of role-reversal in human society: chiefs will become servants; the downtrodden and the oppressed will rule over their former oppressors. The result of all these changes will be a brave new world in which everything fits together in perfect peace and harmony.

What happened when the Christian Gospel, with its eschatological content, came face to face with this traditional Melanesian hope? In retrospect, it is possible to discern a pattern which is common to the history of Christian missions and the history of cargo cults. In those areas where cargo cults occur persistently, there was an initial embracing of the Gospel and the

Christian way of life, apparently because Christianity was thought to offer new solutions to old problems of existence. This initial acceptance of the Gospel was followed by attempts at syncretism; that is, efforts were made to utilize certain features of Christian doctrine and practice in the cargo cults. The final stage in the pattern was either a total integration of Christian or pseudo-Christian beliefs and ritual with the cargo ideology, myth, and ritual (existing in the open and parallel to Christianity, or hidden as a kind of 'underground syncretism'), or a complete rejection of Christianity and its overt and obvious influences.

It seems that at least three factors influenced the reception of the Gospel as I have described it above. The first two factors concern externals, that is, the manner in which the Gospel came.

In many instances, the Gospel was first brought to a new area by men with white skins, or by native evangelists who were sent by men with white skins. This fact assumes some significance when we realize that, in the traditional beliefs of many tribes in Melanesia, a white skin is thought to be a distinguishing characteristic of the returning ancestral dead. Hence, it is not surprising to find that when men with white skins came preaching a message of brotherhood under the rule of Jesus, the Second Adam, the first fruits from the dead, the message was listened to with careful attention, and both the men and the message caused a considerable amount of comment and speculation.

A second factor to be taken into account is that when the white-skinned missionary came preaching the Gospel, he brought with him not only a stimulating message; he brought also seemingly-superhuman skills, amazing knowledge, unbelievable technology, and spectacular material possessions. And he seemed to have access to an unlimited supply of these things. It was almost inevitable that a correlation would be made between the life-style, the knowledge, and the goods of the white missionary on the one hand, and the message which he proclaimed on the other. Anyone with a magico-religious outlook would draw the obvious inference: somewhere in the missionary's message lies hidden the secret, the key to the 'cargo' which he possesses.

A third point to be considered when examining the consequences of the confrontation which took place between traditional and Christian eschatology concerns the nature of Christian eschatology itself. There are some facets of Christian eschatology, some aspects of the theology of hope, and many biblical promises concerning life in the new age, which lend themselves to misunderstanding and misinterpretation, especially in the Melanesian context. The emphasis on the resurrection of Christ, the Second Adam and Head of the new community; the return of this Ancestor Christ to judge the world and to create a new heaven and a new earth; the exhortations to children of the Kingdom to walk as those who are living in the last days and are awaiting the return of their King; the 'feast' parables, and especially the ritual of the Holy Communion in which the Lord's death is remembered until he comes: all these things are easily misunderstood and interpreted in terms of traditional Melanesian beliefs and expectations. Furthermore, the promises given to Christians are easily distorted and explained in a 'cargo' sense. This is particularly so with promises in regard to prayer. Two well-known examples will serve to illustrate the point:

> Ask, and it will be given you; seek, and you will find; knock, and it will be opened to you (Matt. 7:7,8).

Again:

> Seek first his kingdom and his righteousness, and all these things shall be yours as well (Matt. 6:33).

Finally, a re-examination and re-evaluation of Bible translations has revealed that often the words which were chosen to express certain biblical concepts were so loaded with cargoist 'freight' that inevitably they were misunderstood and misused. Unwittingly, misconceptions were encouraged, and even given the stamp of scriptural authority and approval. Kenneth McElhanon gives, as an example, the case in which a word in the local tongue meaning 'white magic' (that is, healing spells and fertility rites) was used to convey the biblical idea of 'blessing'.[5] As a result, wherever the word occurs in the New Testament, it is understood as the practice of white magic. Thus, Paul's words in Romans 15:29 are understood to be: 'I will not come to you empty-handed. I will come to you with the white magic from Jesus'. Other passages, such as Eph. 1:3 and Mark 10:16, are misunderstood in a similar way.

With the advantage of hindsight it is easy to see why a huge communication gap opened up between the preacher of Christian eschatology and the Melanesian hearers. The message was interpreted according to the receptors' own future expectations and hopes. These were decidely this-worldly and directed toward the present and the immediate future. Christianity was seen as a new way of manipulating God in order to effect the rapid realization of the Melanesians' hopes and aspirations for the good life.

Christianity, for its part, failed to recognize the fact that the kind of eschatology it was preaching had little to say to this present life; hence, those who heard it regarded it as an empty eschatology. Furthermore, much Christian preaching distorted, and continues to distort, its own eschatological dimension. With its emphasis on Law-preaching and Law-living, and with its unwillingness to live in the Gospel freedom it sometimes proclaims, the church often obscured the true significance of the dawning of the new age in Christ Jesus.

Sometimes it seemed that the church did not take seriously the victorious hope which it proclaimed, and replaced this hope with a trust in economic development, education, technological advancement, and church organization and structures. Above all, it seems that the church did not take into full account the fact that, in proclaiming its own eschatological beliefs, it was competing with and confronting another set of ideas which were truly indigenous and part of a carefully-integrated system of religious thought and life.

Small wonder, then, that when in 1963 a veteran missionary surveyed the impact of cargo cults on the life of one of the oldest circuits in the Lutheran church, he should write:

> We must conclude, from all the evidence gathered, that the Christian message in the — — — — Circuit was never fully understood . . . Materialism and syncretism took hold of the congregational life and spoiled it before it could develop. The old magic concepts of life were widely retained and mixed up with only partial truths of Christianity.

The point of all this is not to give us the opportunity to sit in smug judgment on the mistakes of others, but to serve as a warning and an incentive to members of the church to learn lessons from the past. Pastors and teachers already at work, as well as seminarians and teacher-trainees, need to be helped to examine carefully the form and content of their own preaching and teaching, lest they unwittingly lend the wrong sort of comfort and aid to those in the grip of cargoism. Effective preaching and teaching in a cargo climate demands of the preacher or teacher that he is so well versed in biblical theology that he moves in it freely and creatively as he preaches and teaches the Word. It is also imperative that the Christian communicator continually reminds himself of the implications of the socio-religious pragmatism of the Melanesians; that he familiarizes himself with the jargon of the cargo cultists; and that he becomes thoroughly acquainted with the double meanings inherent in some theological terms, and with the inbuilt possibilities for syncretism to be found in Christianity and cargoism.

In short, Christian pastors, teachers, and other communicators must assiduously cultivate an *awareness* of the many possibilities which exist for being misunderstood or misinterpreted, or for missing the mark completely in their preaching and teaching. Such awareness, coupled with regular self-examination, should become an integral part of any attempt the church makes to respond creatively to cargo cults.

III

Finally, let me suggest some positive action which the church can take directly on two fronts in its confrontation with cargo cults.

In the first place, the church must remember that cargo cults would not exist without cargo cultists. That is to say, we have to do with people, not merely ideas. Men and women will be weaned away from cargo cults not when they have all their immediate desires granted (for 'cargo' is a symbol for some of the deepest imperatives in Melanesian life), but only when they experience a complete change of heart and mind. Only a radical change in outlook and thinking of people will effect a change in attitude toward cargo cults. A magico-religious outlook; the manipulating of the powers to achieve one's ends; the cardinal importance of the ancestors in the scheme of things: all these are basic elements in cargoism, an integral part of Melanesian philosophy and ideology.

Cargoism can be combated effectively only if a determined effort is made to change the hearts and minds of the Melanesians. This change conceivably could be brought about by immersing Melanesians in secular education and the philosophy of secularism. Marxism, too, has the potential to achieve a total turnabout in the presuppositions, the goals, the thinking, the actions, and the philosophy of life of a people. The Christian church, likewise, has always been the agent for radical change in society from the earliest times onwards. The particular instrument which the church possesses for effecting total change in a person's outlook and thinking, and in the very direction of his life, is the Word of God, consisting essentially of a word of judgment and a word of grace.

If there is one thing that is needed in the churches of Melanesia, it is a far deeper and truer understanding of what is meant by God's word of judgment and God's word of grace, and how these two are to be used effectively in the Melanesian context. As one surveys the past practices of the churches in dealing with cargo cultists, one receives the overwhelming impression that the word of God's judgment has been utilized over and over again, with excommunication being regarded as the ultimate word of judgment. But the word of grace, the Gospel, has not been spoken clearly and consistently. The Gospel has been withheld, or turned into a word that is only conditionally valid, or it has been perverted into another form of Law or a way of life.

The fact is, however, that it is the Gospel alone which, from the Christian point of view, effects the radical change which is necessary to combat cargoism. To excommunicate cargo cultists (which in Melanesia often means exclusion from worship services, and even social ostracization) is to cut them off from the only means the church has of changing their hearts. Excommunication as it is practised in many parts of Melanesia is similar to throwing a sick man out of hospital and telling him that he may return only when he is healthy. Excommunicaton for cargo cultists (for anyone for that matter) is valid only if it achieves that which excommunication is truly intended to achieve, that is, to draw the attention of the Christian community to certain ones who are to be the objects of the community's special concern.

Now, today, the church must learn to make proper use of Law and Gospel — especially the Gospel — in its ministry to cargo cultists. That might seem to be a simplistic solution to a complex problem, but it is essentially the one response the church makes which distinguishes it from responses made by the government and its agencies, or by the social sciences and the humanities. In the final analysis, the proclamation and use of the Law and the Gospel is the only means the church has to carry out its task of turning men away from trust in themselves, or their ancestors, or their secret knowledge, or anything else, to trust in Jesus Christ as Creator, Redeemer, and Lord. But, just because these are the only tools the church has, it is essential that the tools are used properly and appropriately. Christian teachers and preachers must adapt the message to the intellectual wavelength of the hearers. The message must be formulated in such a way, and with such imagery, that it can be fully understood and appreciated for what it is: the Word of the Lord for Melanesians. If the church does not use the Law and the Gospel with all the skill and ingenuity at its disposal, and if it does not communicate Law and Gospel in language which Melanesians will recognize as their own, then there can be no doubt as to the eventual outcome of the confrontation between Christianity and cargoism: cargoism will triumph.

The second positive action the church can take in response to cargo cults and cargo expectations is to continue to be genuinely and practically interested in every aspect of

Melanesian life and culture. The church is already doing this and has always done it. The trouble is, the church's interest in these matters (medical aid, economic development, education, and the like) has been interpreted in cargo terms. This improper interpretation stems, I believe, from the fact that the stunted preaching of Law and Gospel has not effected the desired change in the hearts and minds of those who hear. Consequently, the participation of the church in economic development, health programs, or education is seen not as a necessary fruit of the Gospel, but as the Good News itself. And, since the promise of development or aid seems to attract people to the church far more readily than does the 'foolishness of preaching', the temptation has been for the church itself to substitute these things for the Gospel.

But abuses and possible misuses do not negate the necessity or validity of an action. In seeking to minister to the whole man, the church has been on the right track. But it must strive to do more. This does not necessarily mean that the church must enter into various business enterprises or initiate agricultural development programs and the like. In some situations those things might have to be done. In other situations — perhaps in most situations — the best thing the church can do is to cooperate with other agencies in developing self-help projects within a given community. If it is true that cargo cults represent a search for such non-material things as status, self-respect, integrity, and so forth, then it is not enough for the church to aim at a complete renewal of a man's heart and mind. The church must have something to do and say about the nature and quality of the new life of a man.

The church may offer positive developmental help to a man or a community, and know that it is acting well within its mandate as a church. For the church starts from the conviction that Jesus is Lord in both creation and redemption now. The world and all that is in it — the resources, the technology, the skills — everything belongs to the Lord Jesus and to his Body, the Christian community. This is a present truth. A one-sided emphasis on the life of the world to come, and a refusal to confess and practise the relevance of Christ for this present life, leaves a vacuum which Melanesians abhor. If Christianity will not fill this vacuum, cargoism will.

Christian negativism can have no place in Melanesian Christianity.

In its proclamation and all its activities, the church must sound the note of Christ's lordship in the present life. His lordship is a reality. Salvation is now. At the same time the church cannot hide the already/not-yet tension inherent in the nature of existence in the end-time. Salvation is a present reality, yet its consummation lies in the future. That there is a future; that that future is worth living in and for; and that Jesus Christ is lord of the future: these are the elements of the certain hope which the church may proclaim and live day by day in order to help the cargo cultist burst the bonds of his little world with its inadequate hope. When the Christian says: 'I believe in Jesus Christ', he is confessing his faith that in Jesus Christ the future of the world and of all mankind has dawned. This is the conviction which informs the portrait of Christ painted by the Vatican Council in its *Pastoral Constitution on the Church in the Modern World* (*Gaudium et Spes*, 1,4,45):

God's Word, by whom all things were made, was Himself made flesh so that as perfect man He might save all men and sum up all things in Himself. The Lord is the goal of human history, the focal point of the longings of history and civilization, the centre of the human race, the joy of every heart, and the answer to all its yearnings. He it is whom the Father raised from the dead, lifted on high, and stationed at His right hand, making him Judge of the living and the dead. Enlivened and united in His Spirit, we journey toward the consummation of human history, one which fully accords with the counsel of God's love: 'To re-establish all things in Christ, both those in the heavens and those on earth. (Eph. 1:10).[6]

APPENDIX

Extract from the minutes of the Fifth Synod of the Evangelical Lutheran Church of Papua New Guinea (p 10):

TOK BILIP BILONG KLIAIM KRANKI TINGTING LONG KAGO

Mi wanpela bilong siots bilong Jisas Kraist na mi bilip long tok tru bilong Em na mi tok:

1. God i putim olgeta samting long graun na i stap bilong helpim bodi bilong mi.
2. God i tok, mi mas tingting strong na mekim wok bilong mi, em yet givim mi, na bilong painim kaikai mi mas wok hat na tuhat wantaim.
3. Olsem na mi givim bel long God, na mi pre wantaim mekim wok, na mi tenkyu long blesing bilong God.

* * * * * * * * * * *

4. I nogat rot bilong kisim kago, moni, na arapela samting bilong helpim bodi, long matmat, long maunten, long raun wara na hul.
5. Olsem mi no ken pre long matmat, mi no ken tok nabaut long giaman rot, mi no ken guria nabaut, mi no ken wokim ples long hap bus na mekim prea, mi no ken kamapim driman na plenti arapela pasin i kamap long painim kago. Em i kranki pasin bilong Setan tasol.
6. Sapos mi lukim pasin olsem, na mi harim sampela tok olsem, mi no ken bilip long em, mi givim beksait longen. Em i kranki pasin tasol.
7. Sampela taim wanpela man i tok: mi harim maus bilong engel, no wanpela tok kamap long win na em i harim long taim bilong prea, o long driman em i harim tok olsem profet o wanpela spirit, em giaman bilong Setan tru.
8. Olsem na kain man olsem i laik tok long mekim dispela kain wok mi no ken harim maus bilongen, nogat, mi ken kamapim long kongrigesen na daunim kain kranki tingting olsem. Mi man bilong Siots bilong God nau mi laik sanap strong long tok bilong God nau daunim giaman bilong Setan.

Bikpela Kraist helpim mi na pas wantaim long wok strong na daunim kranki tingting bilong kisim kago. Tru.

NOTES

Introduction

1. This thesis has been developed by my colleague, Willard Burce, in an unpublished paper, 'Cargo Cult: A Response to Continuing Imperatives in Melanesian Culture' (Lae, 1970).

Chapter 1

1. Freerk C. Kamma, 'Messianic Movements in Western New Guinea', *International Review of Missions* XLI (1952), 148-150; Chris Marjen, 'Cargo Cult Movement, Biak', *Journal of the Papua New Guinea Society* I (2, 1967), 62-65; Peter M. Worsley, *The Trumpet Shall Sound*, 2nd augm. ed. (London: MacGibbon and Kee, 1968), 126-130.

2. Kenelm O.L. Burridge, *New Heaven New Earth* (Oxford: Blackwell, 1969), 49-52; Peter M. Worsley, *op. cit.*, 17-31.

3. E.W. Chinnery and Alfred C. Haddon, 'Five New Religious Cults in British New Guinea', *Hibbert Journal* XV (1917), 448-463; Peter M. Worsley, *op. cit.*, 51-54.

4. Peter Lawrence, *Road Belong Cargo* (Melbourne: Melbourne University, 1964), 68-72; Roderic Lacey, 'The Siar Insurrection', *Oral History* IV (1973), 20-24; and a written communication from a former student, the Revd Wesley Kigasung.

5. Peter Lawrence, the Manup-Kilibob myth with its many variations, *op. cit.*, 21-24; 70,71; 75-78; 93,94; 99-103.

6. Peter Lawrence, *op. cit.*, 63-221.

7. E.W. Chinnery and Alfred C. Haddon, *op. cit.*, 460-463; Peter M. Worsley, *op. cit.*, 94-97.

8. Peter M. Worsley, *op. cit.*, 114,115.

9. *ibid.* 54-58.

10. Francis E. Williams, *Orokaiva Magic* (London: Oxford University Press, 1928), 1-99; E.W. Chinnery and Alfred C. Haddon, *op. cit.*, 449-454; Peter M. Worsley, *op. cit.*, 59-74.

11. On the importance of the taro in Orokaiva society, see Erik Schwimmer, *Exchange in the Social Structure of the Orokaiva* (London: C. Hurst, 1973), 111-137.

12. Francis E. Williams, 'The Vailala Madness and the Destruction of Native Ceremonies in the Gulf Division', Territory of Papua *Anthropology Reports No. 4* (Port Moresby: Government Printing Office, 1923); T.H. Kekeao, 'Vailala Madness', *Oral History* VII (1973), 1-8; Dawn Ryan, 'Christianity, Cargo Cults, and Politics Among the Toaripi of Papua', *Oceania* XL (2, 1969), 101-103; Peter M. Worsley, *op. cit.*, 75-92.

13. Francis E. Williams, 'The Vailala Madness in Retrospect' in *The Vailala Madness and Other Essays*, ed. E. Schwimmer (London: C. Hurst, 1975).

14. Dawn Ryan, *op. cit.*, 103.

15. Jean Guiart, 'Forerunners of Melanesian Nationalism', *Oceania* XXII (2, 1951), 86; Peter M. Worsley, *op. cit.*, 148,149.

16. Johannes Flierl, *E-emasang, or a marvellous movement of sanctification in our Lutheran Mission-Church, New Guinea* (1932); Georg Pilhofer, *Die Geschichte der Neuendettelsauer Mission in Neu-Guinea*, Vol. 2 (Neuendettelsau: Freimund, 1963), 159-162; Peter M. Worsley, *op cit.*, 213,214.

17. Freerk C. Kamma, *op cit.*, 150-152; Peter M. Worsley, *op cit.*, 135,136.

18. Freerk C. Kamma, *op. cit.*, 152.

19. Peter M. Worsley, *op. cit.*, 99.

20. *ibid*, 114-121.

21. Alan R. Tippett, *Solomon Islands Christianity* (London: Lutterworth, 1967), 202,203.

22. Peter M. Worsley, *op. cit.*, 103,104.

23. *ibid*, 101.

24. *ibid*, 101-103.

25. Georg Höltker, 'Die Mambu-Bewegung in Neuguinea: ein Beitrag zum Prophetentum in Melanesien', *Annali Lateranensi* V (1941), 181-219; Kenelm O.L. Burridge, *Mambu: A Melanesian Millennium* (London: Methuen, 1960).

26. Kenelm O.L. Burridge, *op. cit.*, 188; *Tangu Traditions* (Oxford: Clarendon, 1969), 403,404.

27. Kenelm O.L. Burridge, *Mambu: A Melanesian Millennium* (London: Methuen, 1960), 197.

Chapter 2

1. Peter Lawrence, *Road Belong Cargo* (Melbourne: Melbourne University, 1964), 92-98.

2. *ibid*, 98-110.

3. F. Henkelmann, 'Kukaik' [sic], unpublished paper, no date (Lae: Martin Luther Seminary Library), 1.

4. Some of the songs are recorded in the Appendix to the paper by F. Henkelmann (see note 3, above).

5. Freerk C. Kamma, 'Messianic Movements in Western New Guinea', *International Review of Missions* XLI (1952), 153-155; Chris Marjen, 'Cargo Cult Movement, Biak', *Journal of the Papua New Guinea Society* I (2, 1967), 64; Peter M. Worsley, *The Trumpet Shall Sound*, 2nd augm. ed. (London: MacGibbon and Kee, 1968), 138,139.

6. Freerk C. Kamma, *op. cit.*, 153.

7. Cyril S. Belshaw, 'Recent History of Mekeo Society', *Oceania* XXII (1, 1951), 1-23; Peter M. Worsley, *op. cit.*, 111-113.

8. Jean Guiart, 'John Frum Movement in Tanna', *Oceania* XXII (3, 1952), 165-175; Peter M. Worsley, *op. cit.*, 153-160.

9. J. Graham Miller, 'Naked Cult in Central West Santo', *Journal of the Polynesian Society* LVII (1948), 330-341.

10. A.C. Cato, 'A New Religious Cult in Fiji', *Oceania* XVIII (2, 1947), 146-156.

11. John Keith McCarthy, *Patrol Into Yesterday* (Melbourne: Cheshire, 1963), 180-182; Leo Scharmach, *Manuale Missionariorum* (Vunapope: Catholic Mission, 1953), 59,60.

12. Leo Scharmach, *op. cit.*, 59.

13. Ben R. Finney, *Big-Men and Business* (Canberra: Australian National University, 1973), 138; Peter M. Worsley, *op. cit.*, 199.

14. Ronald M. Berndt, 'A Cargo Movement in the East Central Highlands of New Guinea', *Oceania* XXIII (1, 1951) 56-65, (2, 1952) 137-158; Ben R. Finney, *op cit.*, 139.

15. Mervyn J. Meggitt, 'The Sun and the Shakers: A Millenarian Cult and Its Transformation in the New Guinea Highlands', *Oceania* XLIV (1 and 2, 1973), 1-37, 109-126.

16. Cf Ph. Gibbs, 'Ipili Religion Past and Present', unpublished Diploma in Anthropology thesis (University of Sydney, 1975), 159.

17. R.F. Maher, *New Men of Papua: A Study in Culture Change* (Madison: University of Wisconsin, 1961); Nancy Hitchcock and Nigel D. Oram, *Rabia Camp: A Port Moresby Migrant Settlement*, New Guinea Research Bulletin No. 14 (Port Moresby and Canberra: Australian National University, 1967), 8-43.

18. Nancy Hitchcock and Nigel D. Oram, *op. cit.*, 40.

19. Colin H. Allan, 'Marching Rule: A Nativistic Cult of the British

Solomon Islands', *Corona* III (3, 1951), 93-100; Glyn Cochrane, *Big Men and Cargo Cults* (Oxford: Clarendon, 1970), 67-96; William Davenport and Gülbün Coker, 'The Moro Movement of Guadalcanal, British Solomon Islands Protectorate', *Journal of the Polynesian Society* LXXVI (1967), 126-129; Colin H. Allan, 'Some Marching Rule Stories', *The Journal of Pacific History* IX (1974), 182-186.
20. William Davenport and Gülbün Coker, *op. cit.*, 127.
21. Paliau Maloat, 'Histori bilong mi taim mi bon na i kamap tede', in Marion W. Ward ed., *The Politics of Melanesia* (Canberra: Australian National University, 1970), 145-161; Theodore Schwartz, *The Paliau Movement in the Admiralty Islands, 1946-1954* (New York: American Museum of Natural History, 1962); B.R. Porai, 'Paliau Maloat', *Oral History* VII (1973), 41-45; Peter M. Worsley, *op. cit.*, 183-194.
22. Theodore Schwartz, 'The Noise: Cargo-Cult Frenzy in the South Seas', *Psychology Today* IV (1971), 51-54.
23. Peter Lawrence, 'The Widening Political Arena in the Southern Madang District', in Marion W. Ward ed., *The Politics of Melanesia* (Canberra: Australian National University, 1970), 93, note 1.
24. Quoted by Louise Morauta in *Beyond the Village: Local Politics in Madang, Papua New Guinea* (Canberra: Australian National University, 1974), 43.
25. Peter Lawrence, *Road Belong Cargo* (Melbourne: Melbourne University, 1964), 217-220. The article in question was entitled 'Yali can not keep his promises'. It was written by the Revd (later Bishop) John Kuder and published in *Ââkesing*, June 1949, last page.
26. Thomas G. Harding, 'A History of Cargoism in Sio, North-East New Guinea', *Oceania* XXXVIII (1, 1967), 12-15.
27. R. Adams, 'The Pitenamu Society', unpublished paper (University of Technology, Lae, 1975), 23-27. Cf also Friedrich Steinbauer, *Melanesische Cargo-Kulte* (Munich: Delp, 1971), 62,63.
28. Michael W. Young, 'Goodenough Island Cargo Cults', *Oceania* XLII (1, 1971), 42-57.
29. William Davenport and Gülbün Coker, *op. cit.*, 132-175; Glyn Cochrane, *op. cit.*, xxii,xxiii.
30. Thomas G. Harding, *op. cit.*, 16-18.
31. R. Adams, *op. cit.*, 27-29, 35-42.
32. Dawn Ryan, 'Christianity, Cargo Cults, and Politics Among the Toaripi of Papua', *Oceania* XL (2, 1969), 112-117.
33. *ibid*, 116.
34. Ben R. Finney, *op. cit.*, 140.
35. *ibid*, 140; Gary B. Blumanthal, 'Cargo Cult Movements', in Theodor Ahrens ed., *A Study of the Lutheran Church in the Bena Area* (Goroka: Melanesian Institute for Pastoral and Socio-Economic Service, 1974), 15.
36. Gary B. Blumanthal, *op. cit.*, 15.
37. Eugene Ogan, 'Cargoism and Politics in Bougainville, 1962-1972', *The Journal of Pacific History* IX (1974), 118-129.
38. *Post-Courier*, July 12, 1976, 1.
39. Eugene Ogan, *op. cit.*, 118-129.
40. Dorothy E.A. Counts, 'Cargo or Council: Two Approaches to Development in North-West New Britain', *Oceania* XLI (4, 1971), 292,293.
41. Hermann Janssen, 'The Story Cult of Kaliai: A Cargo Cult in West New Britain', *Point* I (1974), 13-25; David R. Counts and Dorothy E.A. Counts, 'Apprehension in the Backwaters', *Oceania* XLVI (4, 1976), 294-303.
42. David R. Counts and Dorothy E.A. Counts, *op. cit.*, 294,295.
43. Dorothy K. Billings, 'The Johnson Cult on New Hanover', *Oceania* XL (1, 1969), 13-19.

44. Kenneth A. McElhanon, 'Current Cargo Beliefs in the Kabwum Sub-District', *Oceania* XXXIX (3, 1969), 174-186.

45. Friedrich Wagner, 'Der Cargokult des Luluai von Imom', *Weltmission Heute* 37/38 (1968), 5-19.

46. Ronald F. Schardt, 'The Power of God Versus Cargo Cult', *The Lutheran* IV (2, 1970), 10-13.

47. Louise Morauta, *op cit.*, 39-49 and *passim*; Theodor Ahrens, 'New Buildings on Old Foundations?', *Point* I (1974), 31-36; Garry Trompf, 'The Theology of Beig Wen, The Would-Be Successor to Yali', *Catalyst* VI (3, 1976), 166-172.

48. Louise Morauta, *op. cit.*, 167.

49. L. Hwekmarin, I. Jamenan, D. Lea, A. Ningiga, and M. Wangu, 'Yangoru Cargo Cult, 1971', *Journal of the Papua New Guinea Society* V (2, 1971), 3-27; Michael Knight, 'The Peli Ideal', *Catalyst* V (4, 1975), 3-22; M.S. Kirk, 'Change Ripples New Guinea's Sepik River', *National Geographic* CXLIV (3, 1973), 354-363.

50. P. Gesch, 'National Unity: Village-Style', unpublished paper (1976), 4.

51. Kal Muller, 'Tanna Awaits the Coming of John Frum', *National Geographic* CXLV (5, 1974), 706-715.

52. R. Adams, *op cit.*, 24-27, and my own investigations are my sources of information on Pitenamu.

Chapter 3

1. Kenelm O.L. Burridge reviewing Peter Lawrence's book, *Road Belong Cargo*, in *Man*, vol. 65, no. 92; quoted by Palle Christiansen, *The Melanesian Cargo Cult: Millenarianism as a Factor in Cultural Change* (Copenhagen: Akademisk Forlag, 1969), 127.

2. Jean Guiart and Peter M. Worsley, 'La Répartition des Mouvements Millénaristes en Mélanésie', *Archives de Sociologie des Religions* V (1958), 38-46; quoted by Palle Christiansen, *op. cit.*, 18.

3. See the surveys by Kenelm O.L. Burridge, *New Heaven New Earth* (Oxford: Blackwell, 1969), 97-164; Palle Christiansen, *op. cit.*, 68-109; Glyn Cochrane, *Big Men and Cargo Cults* (Oxford: Clarendon, 1970), 145-158.

4. Friedrich Steinbauer, *Melanesische Cargo-Kulte* (Munich: Delp, 1971), 103-106. He calls his fifth group 'Synoptisch', which I have translated freely as 'eclectic'. In the discussion which follows I have made use of Steinbauer's categories, but not his examples.

5. Vittorio Lanternari, *The Religions of the Oppressed* (New York: Mentor, 1963), 187-189.

6. *ibid*, 254.

7. Hermann Strauss, 'Der Cargokult'. In *Junges Neuguinea: Ein Informationsbuch*, W. von Krause ed. (Neuendettelsau: Freimund, ?1970), 140-157.

8. Palle Christiansen, *op. cit.*, 124-127.

9. Mircea Eliade, 'Cargo Cults and Cosmic Regeneration'. In Sylvia L. Thrupp, ed., *Millennial Dreams in Action* (New York: Schocken Books, 1970), 139-143.

10. Peter M. Worsley, 'Millenarian Movements in Melanesia', *Rhodes-Livingstone Institute* XXI (1957), 23-31; Peter M. Worsley, *The Trumpet Shall Sound*, 2nd augm. ed. (London: MacGibbon and Kee, 1968), 221-256.

11. Peter M. Worsley, *The Trumpet Shall Sound*, 239.

12. Friedrich Steinbauer, *op. cit.*, 107-186.

13. Friedrich Steinbauer, 'Cargo Cults: Challenge to the Churches?', *Lutheran World* XXI (2, 1975), 165.

14. David R. Counts and Dorothy E.A. Counts, 'Apprehension in the Backwaters', *Oceania* XLVI (4, 1976), 299.

15. Brevard Childs, *Myth and Ritual in the Old Testament* (London: SCM, 1968), 29.

16. Peter Lawrence, *Road Belong Cargo* (Melbourne: Melbourne University, 1964), 92-94; Kenelm O.L. Burridge, *Tangu Traditions* (Oxford: Clarendon, 1969), 195-411.

17. Mircea Eliade, *Patterns in Comparative Religions* (London: Sheed and Ward, 1958), 430; cf 416,417.

18. I am indebted to Friedrich Steinbauer, *Melanesische Cargo-Kulte* (Munich: Delp, 1971), 156, for this analysis of the themes in cargo mythology.

19. Kenelm O.L. Burridge, *Tangu Traditions* (Oxford: Clarendon, 1969), 400-402.

20. Peter Lawrence, *op cit.*, 21-24; 70,71; 75-78; 93,94; 99-103.

21. Freerk C. Kamma, 'Messianic Movements in Western New Guinea', *International Review of Missions* XLI (1952), 148-150; Peter M. Worsley, *The Trumpet Shall Sound*, 126-129.

22. Hermann Janssen, Mary Mennis, and Brenda Skinner, *Tolai Myths of Origin* (Milton: Jacaranda, 1973), 93.

23. See the example in Friedrich Steinbauer, *Melanesische Cargo-Kulte*, 191,192.

24. Peter M. Worsley, *The Trumpet Shall Sound*, 235; cf Vittorio Lanternari, *The Religions of the Oppressed* (New York: Mentor, 1963), 240,241.

25. This point was brought to my attention by Mr Waka Busa, a student at Martin Luther Seminary, Lae.

26. Vittorio Lanternari, 'Messianism: Its Historical Origin and Morphology', *History of Religions* II (1962), 63.

27. For example, Ps. 18:27,28; 22:19-21; 34:7,19,20; 55:17,18; 69:1,2; 86:2; 107:13,14; cf Job 13:16.

28. E.M.B. Green, *The Meaning of Salvation* (London: Hodder and Stoughton, 1965), 46-52.

29. Cf Willard G. Oxtoby, 'Reflections on the Idea of Salvation', in *Man and His Salvation*, E.J. Sharpe and J.R. Hinnells eds. (Manchester: Manchester University Press, 1973), 29-37.

30. 'Religions: Fundamental Themes for a Dialogistic Understanding' (1970), 87, 175; quoted by Geoffrey Parrinder, 'The Salvation of Other Men', in *Man and His Salvation*, E.J. Sharpe and J.R. Hinnells eds., 189.

31. Harold W. Turner, 'Tribal Religious Movements — New' in *Encyclopaedia Britannica*, 1974 edn, XVIII, 697-705.

Chapter 4

1. For the purposes of the present study the *corpus Paulinum* is defined as those New Testament letters which, by the consent of the majority of modern scholars, are to be assigned to the apostle Paul or to someone who wrote under the direct influence of the apostle.

2. Cf James M. Fennelly, 'The Primitive Christian Values of Salvation and Patterns of Conversion', in *Man and His Salvation*, E.J. Sharpe and J.R. Hinnells eds. (Manchester: Manchester University Press, 1973), 111-120.

3. Cf Rom. 5:12-21; 1 Cor. 15:20-22; Rom. 8:18-25.

4. Oscar Cullmann, *Christ and Time*, rev. ed. (Philadelphia: Westminster 1964), 115-118.

5. Cf my doctoral dissertation, 'The Return-to-Origins Motif in Pauline Theology . . .' (St Louis: Graduate School of Concordia Seminary, 1973). The exegetical underpinnings for the present chapter may be found in this dissertation. See also the excellent studies in John G. Gibbs, *Creation and Redemption: A Study in Pauline Theology* (Leyden: E.J. Brill, 1971).

6. Hermann Strauss, 'Der Cargokult', in *Junges Neuguinea: Ein Informationsbuch* (Neuendettelsau: Freimund, ?1970), 155.

7. Kenelm O.L. Burridge, *Mambu: A Melanesian Millennium* (London: Methuen, 1960), 172-176.

8. Peter Lawrence, *Road Belong Cargo* (Melbourne: Melbourne University, 1964), 247.

9. Kenelm O.L. Burridge, *op. cit.*, 175.

10. Gernot Fugman, 'Melanesian Concepts of Salvation', unpublished paper (1976), 3. Glyn Cochrane has developed the theme of cargo cults and 'big-men' into a full-length book, *Big Men and Cargo Cults* (Oxford: Clarendon, 1970).

11. Rom. 1:18 - 3:20; 5:12-21; 7:7-11; 8:18-23; 1 Cor. 10:1-11.

12. 1 Cor. 10:1,2; Gal. 3:27,28; Rom. 4:17.

13. Roderic Lacey, 'The Enga World View', *Catalyst* III (2, 1973), 42.

14. Theodor Ahrens, 'Christian Syncretism', *Catalyst* IV (1, 1974), 13.

15. I am endebted to Fugman (see note 10 above) and Ahrens (see note 14, pp 13-15) for this exposition of the concept of *lo* in Melanesia.

16. Rom. 5:14; 1 Cor. 15:22,45. For detailed studies of the Adam/Christ typology see Charles K. Barrett, *From First Adam to Last* (New York: Scribners, 1962), and Robin Scroggs, *The Last Adam: A Study in Pauline Anthropology* (Philadelphia: Fortress, 1966).

17. F.C. Synge, *Philippians and Colossians* (London: SCM, 1951). A meticulous study of the Philippians hymn has been done by Ralph P. Martin, *Carmen Christi: Philippians II, 5-11 in Recent Interpretation and in the Setting of Early Christian Worship* (Cambridge: University Press, 1967).

18. For example, John 3:36; Rom. 8:23,30; Phil. 3:20,21. Cf the discussion by George E. Ladd, 'Apocalyptic and New Testament Theology', in Robert Banks ed., *Reconciliation and Hope* (Exeter: Paternoster Press, 1974), 285-296.

19. Carl E. Braaten, *Christ and Counter-Christ: Apocalyptic Themes in Theology and Culture* (Philadelphia: Fortress, 1972), 129.

20. Gernot Fugman, 'Melanesian Concepts of Salvation', unpublished paper (1976), 3.

21. *ibid*, 3.

22. Isa. 32:15; 44:1-5; Ezek. 37:1-6; Joel 3:1-5.

23. The thoughts of this paragraph are drawn in part from Martin H. Scharlemann, *Healing and Redemption* (St Louis: Concordia, 1965), 58.

24. Martin H. Scharlemann, *The Secret of God's Plan* (St Louis: Concordia, 1970), 45.

25. *ibid*, 45.

Chapter 5

1. Unless the context indicates otherwise, the phrase 'the church' is used in this chapter as a collective term for the various Christian churches in Melanesia. However, my observations and remarks have reference in the first instance to that organization of which I am a member, the Evangelical Lutheran Church of Papua New Guinea.

2. Peter Lawrence, *Road Belong Cargo* (Melbourne: Melbourne University, 1964), 272.

3. See above, 62,63.

4. Gottfried Oosterwal, *Modern Messianic Movements* (Elkhart: Institute of Mennonite Studies, 1973), 9.

5. Kenneth A. McElhanon, 'Appreciating the Possibilities of Tok Pisin', *Catalyst* V (3, 1975), 54. Other examples given by McElhanon, 'Current Cargo Beliefs in the Kabwum Sub-District', *Oceania* XXXIX (3, 1969), 83, are Gen. 12:2,3; 39:5; Acts 3:25,26; Heb. 6:7.

6. Walter M. Abbott, *The Documents of Vatican II* (London-Dublin: Geoffrey Chapman, 1966), 247.

BIBLIOGRAPHY OF BASIC READING

Books

Burridge, Kenelm O.L. *New Heaven New Earth*, Oxford: Blackwell, 1969.

Christiansen, Palle. *The Melanesian Cargo Cult: Millenarianism as a Factor in Cultural Change*, Copenhagen: Akademisk Forlag, 1969.

Gibbs, John G. *Creation and Redemption: A Study in Pauline Theology*, Leyden: E.J. Brill, 1971.

Kamma, Freerk C. *Koreri. Messianic Movements in the Biak-Numfor Culture Area*, The Hague: M. Nijhoff, 1972.

Lanternari, Vittorio. *The Religions of the Oppressed*, New York: Mentor, 1963.

Lawrence, Peter. *Road Belong Cargo*, Melbourne: Melbourne University Press, 1964.

Morauta, Louise. *Beyond the Village: Local Politics in Madang, Papua New Guinea*, Canberra: Australian National University, 1974.

Oosterwal, Gottfried. *Modern Messianic Movements*, Elkhart: Institute of Mennonite Studies, 1973.

Schwartz, Theodore. *The Paliau Movement in the Admiralty Islands, 1946-1954*, New York: American Museum of Natural History, 1962.

Scroggs, Robin. *The Last Adam: A Study in Pauline Anthropology*, Philadelphia: Fortress, 1966.

Sharpe, Eric J. and John R. Hinnells. *Man and His Salvation*, Manchester: Manchester University Press, 1973.

Steinbauer, Friedrich. *Melanesische Cargo-Kulte*, Munich: Delp, 1971.

Williams, Francis E. *Orokaiva Magic*, London: Oxford University Press, 1928.

Wilson, Bryan R. *Magic and the Millennium*, London: Heinemann, 1973.

Worsley, Peter M. *The Trumpet Shall Sound*, 2nd augmented edn, London: MacGibbon and Kee, 1968.

Articles

Ahrens, Theodor. 'Christian Syncretism', *Catalyst*, IV(1), 3-40.

Berndt, Ronald M. 'A Cargo Movement in the East Central Highlands of New Guinea', *Oceania* XXIII(1), 40-65; XXIII(2), 137-158; XXIII(3), 202-234.

Hwekmarin L., I. Jamenan, D. Lea, A. Ningiga, and M. Wangu. 'Yangoru Cargo Cult, 1971', *Journal of the Papua New Guinea Society*, V(2), 3-27.

Janssen, Hermann. 'The Story Cult of Kaliai: A Cargo Cult in West New Britain', *Point* I, 4-28.

Kamma, Freerk C. 'Messianic Movements in Western New Guinea', *International Review of Missions*, XLI, 148-160.

Schwartz, Theodore. 'The Noise: Cargo-Cult Frenzy in the South Seas', *Psychology Today*, IV, 51-54; 102,103.

Steinbauer, Friedrich. 'Cargo Cults: Challenge to the Churches?', *Lutheran World*, XXI(2), 160-172.

Turner, Harold W. 'Tribal Religious Movements — New', *Encyclopaedia Britannica*, 1974 edn, XVIII, 697-705.

Williams, Francis E. 'The Vailala Madness in Retrospect', *The Vailala Madness and Other Essays*, ed. Erik Schwimmer, London: C. Hurst, 1975. (Also available in the Bobbs-Merrill Social Science Reprint Series, No. A-241.)

INDEX TO BIBLICAL REFERENCES

TOPICAL INDEX

Nubos Jengenu 50
Nuliapo Brugue 42

Oosterwal, Gottfried 96,98

Pako 18,22
Paliau Maloat 35
Pascal, Blaise 72
Paul, Apostle 64,65,66,69,70,72,
    75,77,78,79,80,81,82,84,85,86,
    87,100
Pokokoqoro 23
Poro 41

Ronovuro 20,21,30
Russians 53

Sali, Boyamo 50
Sampari 14
Sanop 22
Sariong 40,50
Satan 23,24,46,93,94
Scharlemann, Martin 88
Scharmach, Leo 91,92,95
Selembe 21
Simson 29
Steinbauer, Friedrich 54,58,96
Stephanus Simopjaref 29
Strauss, Hermann 55,56,67
Stückhardt, Wilhelm 17

Tagarab 27,28
Taro (clan) 32
Tieka 30,31
Tikombe 21
Timothy George 34
Toaripi (clan) 20,41
To Kabinana 61
Tokeriu 16,18
Tolai 61
Tommy Kabu 33,34
To Purgo 61
Tuman 60
Turner, Harold W. 63
Tutumang 21

Upikno 23

Virgin Mary 42

Wale-rur'n 47
Wapei 35
Wasjari 21
Worsley, Peter 52,53,57

Yali Singina (see also Lo-bos
    Movement) 18,25,36,37,38,42,
    46,47,83
Yaliwan, Matthias 47,48,49

Zyganek 31

Places
Admiralty Islands 33
Afufuia (Goodenough Island) 38
Angal Village (Bougainville) 43
Apingam (Madang Province) 24
Asaro, Upper (Eastern Highlands)
    41

Banara (Madang Province) 24
Bena Bena (Eastern Highlands) 42
Bethlehem (Irian Jaya) 28
Bibling Ridge (West New Britain)
    43
Bogia (Madang Province) 24,25
Bougainville, see North Solomons
    Province
Buka Island (Solomons) 18,22

Cape Possession (Gulf Province)
    29
Choiseul Island (Solomons) 23

East Sepik Province 47
Eastern Highlands Province 41,97
Enga Province 32,62,74
Erap (Morobe Province) 45
Espiritu Santo Island (New
    Hebrides) 20,30

Fiji Islands 13,15,29,31
Finschhafen (Morobe Province)
    21,37

Geelvinck Bay (Irian Jaya) 14,15
Gitua (Morobe Province) 23
Goodenough Island 38,39
Guadalcanal Island (Solomons) 39
Gulf Province 33,41

Holland 29
Hollandia, see Jayapura
Hurun, Mount, see Turu, Mount

Imom (Morobe Province) 45
Irian Jaya 13,14,15,21,22,25,28,29,
    61

Myths, Movements, and Events

Ain's Cult 32,33

Baigona Cult 18
Baluan Christian Native Church 35
Black King Movement 32

Catholic Church 23,35,45,48,53,93

Eemasang 21

Finongan Movement 45,46

German Wislin Movement 18
Ghost Wind Movement 32

Jehovah's Witnesses 53
John Frum 30,49
Johnson Cult 44,45

Komba Cult 37,38
Koreri 14,15,22
Kukuaik 27,28

Letub Cult 26,27,28,36,38
Lo 46,83
Lo-bos Movement (see also Yali) 46,47,83
Longlong Lotu 42
Lutheran Church 37,41,45,46,53, 93,101

Madang Revolt 17,18
Mangzo Movement, see Skin Guria Movement
Mansren myth 14,15,21,22,61
Manup-Kilibob myth 17,18,25,26, 27,61
Marching Rule 33,34,35,39
Marxism 57,67,102
Melanesian Institute for Pastoral and Socio-Economic Service 97
Methodist Church 23
Moro Custom Movement 33,39,40

Naked Cult 21,30
Napikadoe Navitu 43
Noise, The 35

Pangu Pati 47,50
Peli Association 47,48,49

Pitenamu 38, 41,49,50
Protestants 53

Rai Coast Rehabilitation Scheme 36

Seven Association 49
Seventh Day Adventists 53,96
Siar Insurrection, see Madang Revolt
Skin Guria Movement 37,38,45,50
Stori 43
Story Cult 43,44,59

Tanget Cult 38,40,41,45,50
Taro Cult 18,19
Tuka Cult 15,16
Tutukuval Isukal Asosiesen 45

Vailala Madness 19,20,41
'Vessel of Christ' 31

World War I 13,18
World War II 13,25,26,33,57

A FINAL WORD

To make this volume as up-to-date and correct as possible, the following addenda are submitted.

● Gernot Fugman has now published much of the unpublished material referred to in chapter 4. Hence, note 10 on p 112 should now read: Gernot Fugman, 'Preaching in Melanesia', *Catalyst* VI (4, 1976), 263-266. Note 15 should also be revised to read: I am indebted to Fugman, *op. cit.*, 260-266 . . . Notes 20 and 21 remain unchanged, still referring to unpublished material.

● The following two journal articles can be added to the Bibliography on p 114: Jarvie I.C. 'Theories of Cargo Cults: A Critical Analysis', *Oceania* XXXIV (1), 1-31; XXXIV (2), 108-136. Fugman Gernot. 'Preaching in Melanesia', *Catalyst* VI (4, 1976), 259-269.

● In the Bibliography on p 113, the initial entry under Books was omitted, and must be added because of its importance: Burridge, Kenelm O.L. *Mambu: A Melanesian Millennium*, London: Methuen, 1960.

● It is of interest that in 1977 the Melanesian Institute added two Melanesians to its staff. In the light of this, the statements made on p 97 now happily can be modified.

● The following typographical corrections can also be noted:
p 7, line 5: 'B.H. Schwarz', not 'B.M. Schwarz';
p 20, line 12: 'steamer', not 'steamers';
p 61, line 4: 'sons', not 'son';
p 64, line 22: 'built-in', not 'built-on';
p 78, line 28: 'God's people', not 'God's temple';
p 107, note 3: '458', not '448';
p 118, column 2: 'Sepik River Region', not 'Sepik (Madang Province)'.

DATE DUE
